COME, FOLLOW ME
5

SECOND EDITION

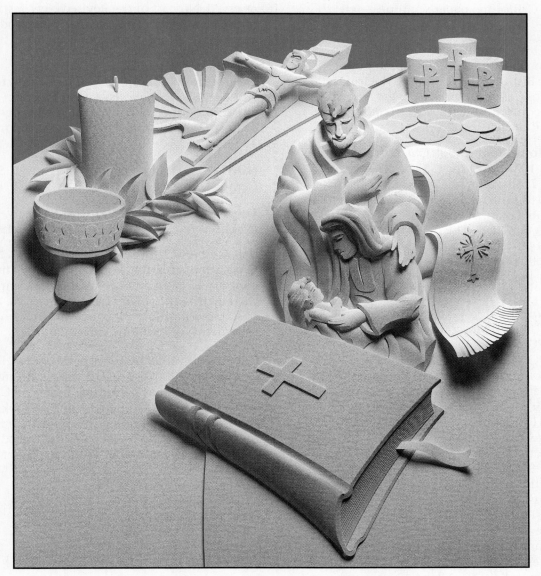

GENERAL EDITORS
Rev. Berard Marthaler, O.F.M. Conv.
Rev. Gerard P. Weber

CONSULTING EDITOR
Irene H. Murphy

RCL *Benziger*

Allen, Texas

Writing Team Jim Bitney, Barbara Malone, Michael McKeefery, Yvette Nelson, Sandra Sella Raas, Charles Savitskas, Margaret Savitskas, Helen Whitaker.

Design and Production Monotype Composition Company, Baltimore, Maryland

Cover Cover Design—Design Office, San Francisco, California; paper sculpture—Jeff Nishinaka

The Ad Hoc Committee to Oversee the Use of the Catechism, National Conference of Catholic Bishops, has found the doctrinal content of *Come, Follow Me, Second Edition,* to be in conformity with the *Catechism of the Catholic Church.*

Illustrations Young Sook Cho: 24–25, 62, 63, 69–70, 96, 102, 116, 126, 132, 200; Kevin Davidson: 7; Susan Jaekel: 24, 53, 56, 78, 104, 105, 178, 181, 182, 186–187, 205; Greg Reynolds: 36; David Rickman: 9, 10, 45, 49, 73, 76, 77, 91, 93, 94, 130, 137, 197; D.J. Simison: 41, 92, 93, 136, 141, 144, 152; Richard Simms: 10–11, 17, 50, 80, 103, 168, 177, 208; Leslie Staub: 173, 174; N.J. Taylor: 60, 113, 128, 153, 154, 175, 176, 184, 192, 194; James Watling: 18, 19, 120, 121, 133

Photographs Art Resource (*The Prophet Elija,* Tretyakov Gallery, Moscow): 129; David Bartruff/FPG International: 33; Leverett Bradley/FPG International: 22; Cameraphoto/ Art Resource: 191; Jose Carrillo/PhotoEdit: 68; Myrleen Cate/Tony Stone Images: 141, 147; Churchill & Klehr/Tony Stone Images: 35; Corbis-Bettman: 16, 166; Gary Conner/PhotoEdit: 112; Cyberimage/Tony Stone Images: 196; Mary Kate Denny/PhotoEdit: 26; Myrleen Ferguson/ PhotoEdit: 8, 134, 140, 141, 160–161; Tony Freeman/PhotoEdit: 22, 135, 140, 169, 170; Robert Frerck/Tony Stone Images: 35; Jeff Greenberg/PhotoEdit: 161; Claude Guillaumin/ Tony Stone Images: 72; Spencer Jones/FPG International: 42; Alan Klehr/Tony Stone Images: 72; Erich Lessing/Art Resource: 29, 115; Stephen McBrady/PhotoEdit: 57; Michael Newman/ PhotoEdit: 26, 60, 75; National Museum of American Art, Washington, D.C.: 27, 56; Nimatallah/Art Resource (Caravaggio, *Supper at Emmaus*): 155; Jon Riley/Tony Stone Images: 21; Scala/Art Resource: 57, (del Sarto, *The Last Supper*) 139, 180; Don Smetzer/Tony Stone Images: 117; Jeremy Walker/Tony Stone Images: 156–157; David Young-Wolff/PhotoEdit: 23, 169

Nihil Obstat Sister Karen Wilhelmy, C.S.J., Censor Deputatus

Imprimatur †Roger Cardinal Mahony, Archbishop of Los Angeles, January 15, 1997

The nihil obstat and imprimatur are official declarations that the work contains nothing contrary to Faith and Morals. It is not implied thereby that those who have granted the nihil obstat and imprimatur agree with the contents, statements, or opinions expressed.

Send all inquiries to:
RCL Benziger
200 East Bethany Drive
Allen, Texas 75002-3804

Visit us at www.RCLBenziger.com

Printed in the United States of America

B5405   ISBN 0-02-655985-4

12 13 14 15 16 • 11 10 09 08 07

This Year I Get To

- Practice new ways of speaking with God in prayer.
- Read about heroes who walked with God.
- Act out stories to make God's Word come alive.
- Learn to see God's footprints in all creation.
- Become a more active member of my parish.

3

TABLE OF CONTENTS ....

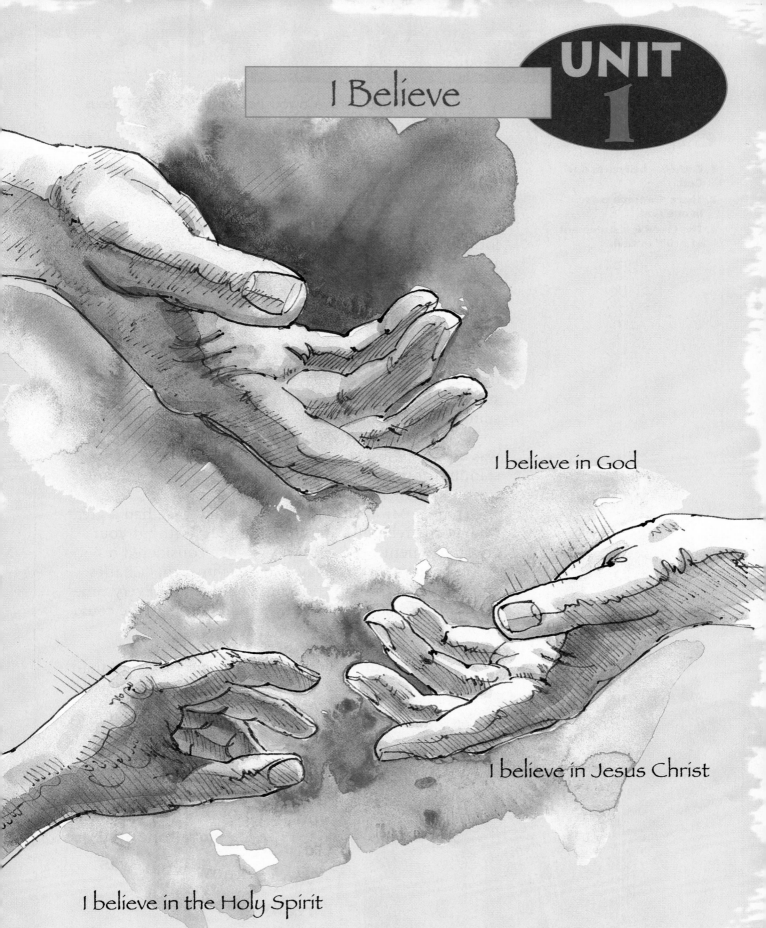

I Believe

I believe in God

I believe in Jesus Christ

I believe in the Holy Spirit

I BELIEVE IN GOD

CONTENT KEYS

1. **Catholics believe in one God.**
2. **There are three persons in one God.**
3. **The Creed is a statement of belief in God.**

> If you believe in your heart that God raised Jesus from the dead, you will be saved.
>
> ROMANS 10:9

WHAT TO BELIEVE?

Jennifer didn't know what to believe. She had heard a lot of bad things about her new fifth grade teacher, Mr. Janeway. If he were as mean as everyone said, this new school year would be a nightmare.

"I heard that he yelled at Charles and Margo and threatened to have them thrown out of school," said Danita.

"I heard that he gives tons of homework, especially over weekends and holidays. Would you believe that six students had to take extra religion classes over the summer?" said Frank.

When Jennifer arrived at school on the first day, she was very nervous. She was surprised to see Mr. Janeway standing at the classroom door before the first bell rang, surrounded by happy sixth graders.

"Thanks, Mr. Janeway," one boy said. "We had a great time at the religion camp this summer. Without your encouragement, we never would have considered it."

Margo gave Mr. Janeway a thumbs-up sign. "Charles and I finished third in the math competition. Every time we wanted to quit, we heard you telling us that we could do it. Thank you."

Jennifer couldn't believe her eyes or her ears.

Apparently there was more to this story than what she had heard. Maybe this would be a good year after all.

Think of a time when you did not know what to believe. What helped you to know what was really true?

I Became a Christian

My name is Gallia. I am twelve years old. My father sells wheat and barley in a little shop in Rome. Four years ago, our home burned down, along with many other homes around us. It was terrible! Then some Christian people who lived in another part of the city took us in and helped us rebuild.

We were amazed by their kindness. We wondered why they helped us. They said that Jesus taught them to help anyone in need. That's when my parents and I decided that we wanted to follow Jesus, too. One of our Christian friends presented us to the community. We began the catechumenate, a time of study and prayer in preparation for Baptism.

I FOLLOWED THE WAY

As my parents and I prepared for Baptism, we learned more about how Christians live and follow Jesus. As we learned, we began to act as Christians. We turned away from other gods. We helped widows and people who were poor. We prayed. And the people in the community, who had become like part of our family, prayed for us.

Finally, the day of our baptism, the Easter Vigil, arrived. I was so excited I could barely control myself!

1. **What led Gallia and her family to become Christians?**
2. **What can you do to lead others to become Christians?**

I Do Believe

When we arrived at the celebration of the Easter Vigil, the whole community was waiting for us with lighted candles. After the Scripture readings, my parents were baptized. Then it was my turn. My heart was pounding.

"Do you believe in God the Father almighty?"

I answered, "I do believe." Then I was lowered into the baptismal pool. The water was warm.

"Do you believe in Christ Jesus, the Son of God, who was born of the Holy Spirit and the Virgin Mary, who was crucified in the days of Pontius Pilate, and died, and rose the third day living from the dead, and ascended into heaven, and sat down at the right hand of the Father, and will judge the living and the dead?"

I answered proudly, "I do believe." Again I was lowered into the water.

"Do you believe in the Holy Spirit, in the holy catholic church, and the resurrection of the body?"

With a clear, strong voice, I said again, "I do believe." That time the water covered me. I stood up, dripping and smiling.

Now I am a Christian, a true follower of Jesus!

I Believe...

Gallia made a profession of faith. In the space, write three truths showing what you believe about God.

1.

2.

3.

LEARNING TO TRUST

In the space, write about a time when you had to trust someone to help you with an important project. What did you learn from this experience?

TRUST GOD

Hi. It's me again. Gallia. Preparing for Baptism was not easy for me or my family. I was worried about not being ready. When I confided in my teacher, she said, "Listen to what Jesus said."

Look at the birds of the sky. They don't have a worry in the world. The loving Father takes care of them. Now, the truth is, the heavenly Father cares more about you than a whole flock of birds. God wants you to trust. God didn't make you for worry and fear, but for faith and trust.

Based on MATTHEW 6:25–26

FATHER, SON, AND HOLY SPIRIT

Before we were baptized, the deacon told me, "Gallia, it will take you several years to become a Christian." I studied for three years before my baptism. The most difficult thing for me to understand was the Blessed Trinity. What does it mean to say that there is only one God, who is Father, Son, and Holy Spirit?

I believe that God is a loving Father who cares for me. I just look around and see everything that God made: the sun and stars, the hills and sea—and me!

I believe that Jesus is God and man. I learned that Jesus was born of the Virgin Mary. He taught about the Father and suffered and died to save all people from sin and death. Knowing that Jesus rose from the dead and is with the Father in Heaven makes me feel good. I look forward to the time when Jesus comes again in glory. He said no one knows when that day will come.

I believe that the Holy Spirit was sent by God, as Jesus promised, as a helper and guide for the Church. The Spirit of God was surely working through the Christians who helped my family.

I am glad that God gave me the gift of faith. With faith, I can know God and believe what the Church teaches. I can believe because I trust Jesus.

DID YOU KNOW?

People wear shamrocks on Saint Patrick's Day because Saint Patrick used a three-leaf clover to teach the people of Ireland about the Blessed Trinity.

Throughout the ages, people have used many symbols to explain the Trinity. The three gold circles, for instance, stand for the Father, Son, and Holy Spirit. The three points form a triangle to show that the three persons are one God.

FOLLOWING Jesus

You can follow Jesus by doing what he asked: be kind to people, care for the sick, and treat everyone with respect. When you put what you believe into action, you tell other people how important Jesus is to you. Your actions give witness to who Jesus is. By your example, you can lead other people to follow Jesus, too.

THE CREED

The words that Gallia said at her Baptism sound very much like the Apostles' **Creed** that you say today. It is called the Apostles' Creed because it expresses the same beliefs of the church that the Apostles taught. When you pray the creed, you are saying that you hold the same beliefs as those handed down by the Apostles.

Over time, different forms of the Creed developed. Some were long and some were short, but all professed the Church's belief in the Holy Trinity. In A.D. 325, the bishops of the world met at the Council of Nicaea and agreed on a way to express what the Church believes. Today the Nicene Creed is proclaimed by Christians throughout the world.

Like the Apostles' Creed, the Nicene Creed praises the work of the Father, Son, and Holy Spirit. Whenever Christians pray this Creed, they are united in faith with Christians of all times, past and present. When you pray, you praise God and proclaim what you believe. When you act as a Christian and live as Jesus told you to live, you are acting as a **witness** to the truth of his message.

1. **What is the importance of the Nicene Creed?**
2. **Besides praying the Creed, tell one way you can give witness to your belief in God.**

MAKING A DIFFERENCE

Gallia's family learned a whole new way of life because of their belief in Jesus. Your life will be different, too, the more you try to follow Jesus. In the space provided, respond to each of the following statements with one example of how following Jesus will make a difference in how you live.

Following Jesus Will Make a Difference in the Way I:

Talk to God

Live as a member of my family

Work and play at school

Make the world a better place

PROFESSION OF FAITH

To witness your desire to follow Jesus, renew the promises of your own baptism using the questions and answers on page 10 or by praying the Creed on page 235.

WITH YOUR FAMILY

Name one thing you can do as a follower of Jesus today to make a difference in your family. What do you need to do to make this one thing happen? What can you do to make this one thing happen now?

CATHOLICS BELIEVE

1. There is only one God.
2. There are three Persons in the one God: Father, Son, and Holy Spirit. This belief is known as the doctrine of the Blessed Trinity.
3. A creed is a statement of belief. Christians proclaim the Apostles' and Nicene Creed.

SUNDAY MASS

The Nicene Creed is said aloud each Sunday after the Scripture readings and the homily. When you stand to pray it this week, remember that the words you say express what you believe to be true. Think about how it tells what you believe about God the Father, Son, and Holy Spirit.

KNOW

For each word in Column A, choose the best description from Column B.

Column A

b 1. Witness
f 2. Apostles' Creed
d 3. Catechumenate
c 4. Blessed Trinity
a 5. Easter Vigil
e 6. Nicene Creed

Column B

a. The celebration held on the night before Easter Sunday.
b. To express or live out your beliefs in a public way.
c. God the Father, Son, and Holy Spirit.
d. A time of study and prayer before Baptism.
e. The profession of faith Catholics pray at Mass.
f. A prayer that expresses the beliefs taught by the Apostles.

2 CREATOR AND FATHER

CONTENT KEYS

1. **God is the Creator of all.**
2. **God can be seen in creation.**
3. **God continues to care for all creation.**

God created plants, animals, and people so that you could discover God in the beauty and wonder of all that was made.

From ROMANS 1:20

THROUGH GOD'S EYES

Imagine that you are an astronaut, floating in zero gravity as you circle the earth. Look out the window and describe what you see. How does this view make you feel?

Seeing the earth from space is almost like seeing it through God's eyes. From space you can see the vastness of creation and wonder at the greatness of the Creator of it all.

1. What does the view of earth from space tell you about God?

2. What do you see from this view that shows that God cares for creation?

QUESTIONS ABOUT CREATION

You've been chosen to conduct an interview with God about the mystery of creation. You are to submit two questions in writing. God will get back to you with the answers. What two questions about creation would you ask? Use the space below to compose your questions.

You are not the first person to wonder about creation. People have always asked questions about what God has made; that is, about everything that exists. If you could actually conduct a face-to-face interview with God, you could have your questions answered directly. Until then, you will have to search for answers in the world around you. Two people who found remarkable answers to their questions by careful study are Niels Stensen and Gregor Mendel.

1.

2.

ANSWERS IN A GARDEN

Father Gregor Mendel wondered why some of the pea plants were tall, while others were short. Why some have smooth pods, while other pods were wrinkled? To Father Mendel, this was a puzzle worth solving.

Mendel, an Augustinian priest who lived from 1822 to 1884, carefully conducted a two-year experiment, carefully planting peas, and then studying the results. After studying more than one hundred thousand pea plants, Father Mendel concluded that the size of the plant and the shape of the pod were controlled by a code within the plant. Father Mendel had discovered genetic codes—the codes that control every living thing. His questions led him to discover a secret of creation.

Following Jesus

Curiosity leads you to ask questions, to wonder, and to closely examine God's world. The answers you find can help you grow closer to God. Use your curiosity to find out more about the world you live in.

WRITTEN IN STONE

Niels Stensen, who lived from 1638 to 1686, loved the mountains of Norway. He was also fascinated by the many different layers of rock he saw there: sandstone, granite, shale. How had these layers been formed? How could fossils of fish embedded in the rock be found thousands of feet above sea level?

Stensen searched and questioned until he found answers. His research established the foundation for the modern study of geology and fossils.

Stensen was also curious about the human body. He made many medical discoveries.

Soul: When people put their hearts and souls into a game, it means they've got into their effort. The soul is the part of you that God made to live forever.

Through the study of the body, he saw the dignity of the **soul**. Stensen said, "Through studying both the body and soul, I have come to the knowledge of their author, God." In his search, Stensen discovered God—the Creator, the maker of everything—at the heart of creation.

ANSWERS IN HEAVEN

Imagine a conversation between Gregor Mendel and Niels Stensen meeting in heaven. Act it out with one of your friends.

Stensen: How can people look at the world, and not see the face of the Creator? God is right before their eyes.

Mendel: Yes, of course, but there is so much more they can't see. God's plan of Creation continues, hidden within every creature.

Stensen: *(Brushing his mustache with his fingers)* You know, I am still learning about the way God made us. It makes me love God all the more.

Mendel: *(No longer able to control his joy)* I know! I know! It will take us forever to understand everything!

Stensen: *(Turning to you)* And you, my friend, what have you discovered about God from creation?

Your Response ■

Answer Niels Stensen's question.

Name one thing about creation that tells you about God.

CREATOR AND FATHER

Although the afternoon was quite warm, a large crowd of people continued to follow Jesus. Seeking shade, he led them up the hillside and sat down. Across the valley they could see green fields and rolling hills, golden in the sun. The long meadow grass rustled in the breeze. Here and there, patches of bright wild flowers bloomed.

Jesus pointed to the flowers in the field, and said this:

Learn from the way the wild flowers grow. They do not work or spin, yet they are more beautiful than a king in his finest clothes. If God so cares for the flowers of the field, which bloom for just one day, how much more will your heavenly Father provide for you?

From MATTHEW 6:28, 30

A NEW STORY

Jesus' story of the wild flowers tells about God's love for all of creation. If Jesus wanted to tell about God's love today, he might use a different example. Write a short story that would show your friends that God cares for them. Act out your short story.

A Caring Creator

All of creation is special because it was made by God. All of creation honors God by doing God's work. Sometimes people do not do the work that God wants them to do. People have the freedom to say "no" to God. Jesus told a parable about a young man who said "no" to his father. Find three things in this story that tell you something about God the Father.

A man had a lazy son who would rather play than work on the farm. This lazy son asked his father for money. When he received it, the son took the money, went off, and quickly spent it all. When he ran out of money, the young man ended up living on the street. Broke, starving, and embarrassed, the son decided to go back home. He hoped his father would take him back as an employee. Was he ever in for a surprise!

The son stopped at the top of the last hill before home, afraid to go any further. His father had every reason to laugh in his face or to say he was a no-good worthless son. Looking to the house, he saw his father running up the road toward him, waving his arms and shouting. The son could only fall to his knees and bow his head in shame. He could not bear to look at the anger in his father's eyes.

But there was no anger in the father's eyes, only joy. He grabbed the youth, hugged him, and told him how much he had been missed. Then his father threw a party in celebration of his son's safe return. This was not at all what the son had expected.

A Modern-Day Parable

Read the story of the forgiving Father in the Bible *(Luke 15:11–32)*. Then in your own words, share ideas about how you would tell the story as if it were happening today.

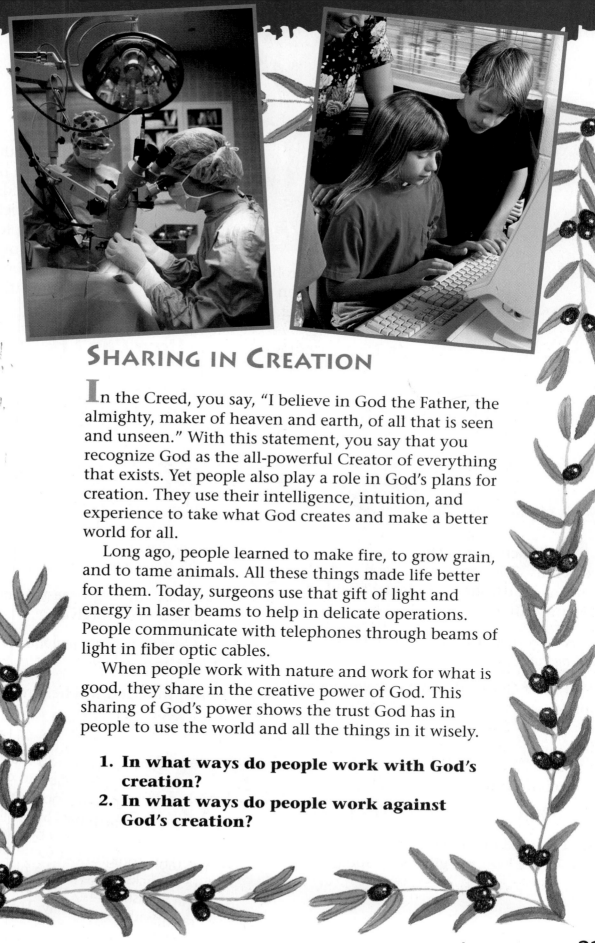

SHARING IN CREATION

In the Creed, you say, "I believe in God the Father, the almighty, maker of heaven and earth, of all that is seen and unseen." With this statement, you say that you recognize God as the all-powerful Creator of everything that exists. Yet people also play a role in God's plans for creation. They use their intelligence, intuition, and experience to take what God creates and make a better world for all.

Long ago, people learned to make fire, to grow grain, and to tame animals. All these things made life better for them. Today, surgeons use that gift of light and energy in laser beams to help in delicate operations. People communicate with telephones through beams of light in fiber optic cables.

When people work with nature and work for what is good, they share in the creative power of God. This sharing of God's power shows the trust God has in people to use the world and all the things in it wisely.

1. **In what ways do people work with God's creation?**
2. **In what ways do people work against God's creation?**

WORKING WITH GOD

As a trusting Father, God asks you to take a hand in the work that needs to be done to create a better world for all people.

In the box below, describe a problem you see in your school, neighborhood, or town. Then tell one way that you can work with God to make it better.

What's the Problem?	How Can I Help?

OUR FATHER

Read each part of the Lord's Prayer carefully. Then read what each part means. Add your own prayer, aloud or silently, after each part.

Our Father, who are in Heaven, hallowed be your name.

I greet God with words of wonder and praise.

Your kingdom come, your will be done on earth as it is in heaven.

I commit myself to God's plan.

Give us this day our daily bread

I depend on God for everything; even the bread I eat is a gift from God.

and forgive us our trespasses, as we forgive those who trespass against us.

I ask God for forgiveness. I am called to forgive as God forgives.

And lead us not into temptation, but deliver us from evil.

I trust that God will help me choose what is good.

WITH YOUR FAMILY

In the Lord's Prayer, you ask God to give you the food you need each day. Share in God's work by volunteering to set the table tonight. Put some bread, bread sticks, or rolls on a nice plate or in a basket. Pray the Lord's Prayer with your family. Then pass the bread.

CATHOLICS BELIEVE

1. God created everything.
2. God is seen in creation.
3. Like a loving father, God continues to care for all creation.

KNOW

Determine whether the question is true or false.

T F   1. Catholics believe that God created the world and everything in it.

T **F**   2. Father Mendel taught that it was wrong to ask questions about creation.

T F   3. Jesus taught people to think of God as a loving father.

T **F**   4. Niels Stensen understood more about God from his study of creation.

T **F**   5. God created the world and then forgot about it.

T F   6. Human beings can work with God to make the world a better place.

SUNDAY MASS

ONE LORD, JESUS CHRIST

CONTENT KEYS

1. Jesus is true God and true man.
2. Jesus is God's son
3. Mary is the Mother of God.

At the name of Jesus every knee should bend, and every voice proclaim that Jesus Christ is Lord.

From PHILIPPIANS 2:10–11

WATCH FOR A SIGN

Josh was hungry. "Mom, is there any homemade pudding left from last night?" Josh asked. Not waiting for his mom to answer, Josh headed for the refrigerator. When he was about to open the door, he noticed the plaque hanging there. What's this? thought Josh.

What do you think the plaque says?

WHO IS THIS JESUS?

Here is a play for you to act out with your friends.

Act One: Spread the News

It's nine o'clock on a warm summer morning. The streets of Jerusalem are more crowded than usual.

Narrator: Loud voices are coming from the second floor windows of a building near the south gate.

Voices: *(offstage)* Hallelujah! Praise the Lord! Hallelujah!

(People in street)

Voice 1: Do you hear that noise?

Voice 2: What is going on up there?

Voice 3: What does this mean?

Woman: *(Shouting)* Someone is coming out of the building!

Peter: (*In a loud voice*) Listen to me! Jesus of Nazareth was a man sent to you by God. He performed mighty deeds and wonders that God worked through him in your midst. You had this man killed! You already know this. What you do not know is that God has raised him up!

(*Voices calling out from crowd*)

Voice 1: He's crazy!

Voice 2: Could this be true?

Voice 3: Listen, listen to him!

Peter: God has raised this very Jesus from death, and we are all witnesses to this fact. This Jesus is the Lord and Messiah! Be baptized, every one of you, in the name of Jesus Christ.

Narrator: That day, many people were baptized by the Apostles and became followers of Jesus. But they still had many questions.

(*Voices calling out from the crowd*)

Voice 1: Where did this Jesus come from?

Voice 2: What did he teach?

Voice 3: Jesus' disciples will know! Let's ask them.

Narrator: All day long, and for many days afterwards, the disciples shared all they knew and remembered about Jesus. Years passed. Eventually, the stories and sayings of Jesus were written down.

Act Two: The Story Continues

Family gathered for Sunday Mass. The pastor is speaking to the congregation.

Pastor: Listen as I read you a story from Jesus' life. This story was recorded by Mark. Mark calls his story of Jesus' life the Gospel, or Good News of Jesus.

Narrator: Four books tell the Gospel of Jesus: Matthew, Mark, Luke, and John, the four **evangelists.**

Child: How can I learn about Jesus?

Mother: You can read and listen to the Gospel. Jesus' message was written there by the Church with God's help.

Based On ACTS 2:4–41

SPECIAL WORDS

The words *angel* and **evangelist** come from the Greek word for messenger. An angel is a messenger from God. An evangelist is one who brings good news.

W.H.Johnson

WHAT'S IN A NAME?

Look at the pictures of Jesus on these two pages. In the space provided, describe what you learn about Jesus from each picture.

NAME HIM JESUS

In the sixth month, the angel Gabriel was sent from God to a town of Galilee called Nazareth, to a virgin betrothed to a man named Joseph, of the house of David, and the virgin's name was Mary.

LUKE 1:26–27

The message that the angel Gabriel brought to Mary was the message that the people of Israel so desperately awaited. The time had come. The waiting was over. God's promise was about to be fulfilled. Mary was to bear a son, the Savior promised by God. The angel Gabriel told Mary to name her child Jesus.

The name Jesus is a form of the common Hebrew name *Yeshua,* or *Joshua.* The name means "God will save." Jewish families often named their sons Yeshua to keep alive God's promise to send a savior.

TITLES IN THE CREED

The titles of Jesus are also like pictures of Jesus. Each one tells something about who Jesus is. The Creed contains three titles of Jesus—Lord, Christ, and Son of God.

You show reverence when you give respect and honor to God. You honor God by showing respect for all creation. Name calling and put-downs can become a bad habit. Make a promise to use the names and nicknames of friends and family members with respect.

- The title *Lord* means "a powerful ruler." Early Christians used this title to proclaim that the Risen Jesus is the ruler of all creation.
- The title *Christ* comes from the Hebrew word *Messiah,* meaning "the anointed one of God." When he walked on earth, Jesus was known as "Jesus of Nazareth" or "Jesus, son of Joseph."
- The title *Son of God* expresses the belief that Jesus—together with the Father and the Holy Spirit—is God. He is one with the Father and the Spirit. Jesus was with the Father before the world was created.

HE BECAME MAN

In the Creed you profess, "By the power of the Holy Spirit he was born of the Virgin Mary and became man." These few words explain a great deal about who Jesus was.

- Jesus was the Son of God, conceived by the power of the Holy Spirit.
- Jesus was human, with a human mother. He did not simply look like a man—he was a man. He had a physical body that felt hunger and thirst, and he laughed and suffered. He had a human mind that asked questions and learned many facts and skills.

Although Jesus was fully human, he was like no other human being. Jesus had a human mother, Mary, but he had no human father.

Jesus was true God and true man. He had both a divine and human nature. Jesus was both God and man, an important mystery of the Christian faith.

THE FIRST DISCIPLE

Mary was the first person to hear and accept the Good News. That is why Mary is called the first disciple. She accepted God's messenger and agreed to God's plan for her life. When Jesus was dying on the cross, he looked down at his mother, Mary, and his beloved disciple. Jesus said to them, "This is your mother. This is your son" *(John 19:26–27)*. Since then, Catholics claim Mary as their mother, too. Honor is paid to Mary because she is the Mother of Jesus. Mary is called Blessed Mother, Blessed Virgin, Mother of God, and Our Lady. People also honor Mary as the Health of the Sick, the Refuge of Sinners, and the Help of Christians.

Catholics show their devotion to, or faithful love for, Mary through prayer and actions. During the year, the Church celebrates many feasts of the Blessed Mother. The feasts of Mary and prayers to Mary always show love and honor to Jesus.

1. **What do names and titles tell about a person?**
2. **What does the name *Jesus* mean?**
3. **Why is Jesus known as the Christ?**

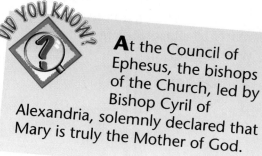

DID YOU KNOW?

At the Council of Ephesus, the bishops of the Church, led by Bishop Cyril of Alexandria, solemnly declared that Mary is truly the Mother of God.

What Do You See?

Choose one title for Jesus and one title for Mary. Make a symbol that shows what this title means to you.

IN JESUS' NAME

The name of Jesus deserves respect. You can show respect for Jesus' name by using it only in prayer. Using Jesus' name in anger or as a joke shows disrespect.

In the space provided, describe how you can show respect for Jesus' name in each of the following situations.

1. When someone accuses you of telling a lie.

2. Before a big game.

3. When you are asked to do something you don't want to do.

4. When you've lost something important to you.

HAIL MARY

One way to honor the names of Jesus and Mary is to pray the Hail Mary. The first part of the prayer consists of the words that the angel Gabriel and Mary's cousin Elizabeth spoke to Mary. The second part of the prayer uses the ancient title Mother of God and asks Mary to care for you as a mother, too. Pray the Hail Mary quietly. Think about the words as you pray them.

Hail Mary, full of grace, the Lord is with you.

Blessed are you among women, and blessed is the fruit of your womb, Jesus.

Holy Mary, Mother of God, pray for us sinners, now and at the hour of our death. Amen.

WITH YOUR FAMILY

Around the dinner table this evening, ask each member of your family to share a favorite name or title for Jesus. Be ready to share your favorite one with them.

▼ REVIEW CHAPTER 3 . . . .

CATHOLICS BELIEVE

1. Jesus Christ is true God and true man.
2. Jesus is the Son of God and Savior of the world.
3. Mary is the Mother of God and your Mother, too.

KNOW

Complete each sentence by choosing the correct word or words.

1. The name Jesus means (God will save, God with us).
2. Matthew, Mark, Luke, and John are called the four (evangelists, bishops).
3. The name (Gospel, Parable) is given to the four New Testament books that tell about Jesus.
4. The early Christians gave Jesus many different (gifts, titles).
5. Jesus received the title *Christ*, which means ("anointed one," "son of Joseph").
6. The Council of Ephesus solemnly declared that Mary is the Mother of (God, John).

SUNDAY MASS

At every Mass, a portion of one of the four Gospel accounts is read as part of the Liturgy of the Word. Listen for the name of the evangelist whose Gospel is read this Sunday. What does this Sunday's Gospel story tell about Jesus?

THE MYSTERY OF FAITH

CONTENT KEYS

1. **Jesus modeled a life of service.**
2. **Jesus is the Savior of the world.**
3. **Jesus will come again in glory.**

Amen, amen, I say to you, unless a grain of wheat falls to the ground and dies, it remains just a grain of wheat; but if it dies, it produces much fruit.

JOHN 12:24

IT'S NOT FAIR!

Peter was angry. He stomped into the house, slammed the door, and threw his comic books on the floor. This seemed like a good time for a father and son chat, his dad thought.

"What's the matter, son?" his dad asked.

"It's just not fair, Dad. I've been working on my science project on snakes for three weeks. I completed my report, and Mom helped me build my model. On the way to school, the model fell and broke. Miss Hardy said I had to make a new model. I already built one model. Why do I have to build another one? It's just not fair!"

You Decide

On the chart below, react to Peter's problem. Then describe a time when you were faced with a situation that was just not fair.

	What Happened?	Was It Unfair?	What Could Have Been Done?
Peter's project			
My story			

Give one example of how failure can lead to an even bigger success.

A Different Way

Jesus told a story.

A vineyard owner hired workers to tend the grapes. Some of the workers started early in the morning, some started at lunch, and some started late in the afternoon. At sundown, the workers gathered at the well to have a drink of water, wash, and collect their wages.

The owner of the vineyard gave each worker the amount of money that had been promised. Each worker received the same amount of money. The workers who had started early in the day thought this was unfair.

"We worked all day in the hot sun. Some of these others worked only an hour in the cool evening. You have cheated us!" the workers said.

"How have I cheated you, my friends?" the owner replied. "I have paid you what I promised. Am I not free to be generous with these other workers?

"That is what the kingdom of God is like."

Based on Matthew 20:1–15

What do you think? Was the landowner unfair to the first workers?

Speaking in Parables

The story of the generous owner is a parable. Jesus often taught with these short stories that use ordinary images to make a bigger point.

These teachings of Jesus were surprising to many. When people understood the point of the parables, many considered them unfair. Yet through these teachings, Jesus revealed some of the greatest mysteries of life. If you want to gain something important, you have to give something else up in return.

WHO IS THIS MAN?

At first, Jesus was very popular in Galilee. Everywhere he went, crowds gathered to see this new prophet who had such great power. He healed sick people. He fed large groups with a small amount of food. He even told people that their sins were forgiven.

Jesus taught in parables, and people did not always understand his teachings. Jesus said, "Blessed are the poor." But poor people were often hungry and homeless. Being poor didn't seem like much of a blessing. Jesus also said, "Blessed are those who suffer." Being in pain didn't seem like very much fun either. What did Jesus mean by these teachings?

Sometimes Jesus' teachings were very difficult to accept. Speaking to a crowd of people, Jesus offered them lifegiving bread.

> *Amen, amen, I say to you, whoever believes has eternal life. I am the bread of life. I am the living bread that came down from heaven; whoever eats this bread will live forever; and the bread that I will give is my flesh for the life of the world.*
>
> JOHN 6:47–48, 51

Upon hearing this, people were shocked. Even Jesus' closest friends were surprised by this talk: "This saying is hard; who can accept it?" *(John 6:60).* As a result of this teaching, many of Jesus' disciples left him.

THE KINGDOM IS LIKE

Read one of the following parables. Draw a modern image of what the kingdom of God is like.

Matthew 13:18–23   Matthew 13:47–50

Matthew 13:24–30   Matthew 18:12–14

Matthew 13:33

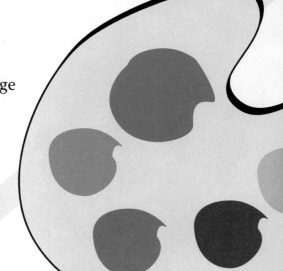

CHRIST HAS DIED

Jesus said, "Whoever would save his life, must lose it." Many people found this saying hard to understand. Jesus answered this riddle with his own life. He suffered and died, he rose from the dead, and he ascended into heaven. These actions of Jesus are at the heart of the Christian faith. In Jesus' death and resurrection, you too are saved from sin and death.

Each year, people journey to Jerusalem to remember Jesus. These people are pilgrims, visiting places important to their faith. Their journey is called a pilgrimage. In the Middle Ages, people who had completed the long, dangerous journey to the Holy Land proudly wore a palm leaf from Jerusalem in their hat or on their cloaks as badges of honor.

You can make a pilgrimage by remembering the events of Jesus' Passion.

+ Jesus' passion begins in the garden of Gethsemani. Read Mark 14:32–42. What happened to Jesus in this garden?

+ After Jesus is arrested in the garden, he is placed on trial—first by the Jewish high court, the Sanhedrin, and next, by Pilate. What thoughts do you have for Jesus as he faces people who wish to put him to death?

+ Jesus is sentenced to death by Pilate. He is tortured by soldiers and forced to carry his own wooden cross. He falls several times along the way, where he is comforted by followers. A stranger named Simon helps Jesus carry his cross.

+ Jesus is nailed to the cross and dies after much suffering. He is buried in a tomb.

Christians believe that Jesus offered his life to free the world from the power of sin. It is this act of selfless love that is remembered each Lent in the reading of the Passion. Millions of pilgrims follow Jesus in Jerusalem or in their parish churches, where they pray the stations of the cross. Many millions more journey with Jesus by praying the Sorrowful Mysteries of the Rosary.

CHRIST HAS RISEN

DID YOU KNOW?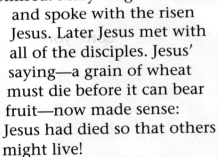

The image of a lamb holding a banner is a sign of the Paschal Mystery—Jesus dying, rising to new life, and returning as he had promised. The word *paschal* comes from the Jewish feast of the Passover. Passover celebrates God's great deeds in leading the Israelites out of slavery in Egypt into freedom in the Promised Land. As part of this feast, every family offered a lamb to God as a sacrifice of love.

If Jesus' story had ended with his death and burial, he might have been forgotten. But the last words in the Gospels are not, "They blocked the tomb with a large stone." There is much more to Jesus' story.

The burial custom in Jesus' day was to wash the body and to anoint it with perfume. These last acts of kindness showed love and respect for the person who had died. When Jesus was buried, his body was placed in the tomb unwashed and unanointed. There was no time to complete these acts before the Jewish Sabbath began on Friday at sundown. On the first day of the new week (Sunday), Mary Magdalene, Salome, and Mary the mother of James, all disciples of Jesus, came to the tomb to anoint Jesus with perfume and spices.

The women were shocked to find an empty tomb. What had happened to Jesus? An angel told them that Jesus had risen as he had promised. Mary Magdalene met and spoke with the risen Jesus. Later Jesus met with all of the disciples. Jesus' saying—a grain of wheat must die before it can bear fruit—now made sense: Jesus had died so that others might live!

After the resurrection, Jesus' disciples understood that Jesus was the Son of God, the long-awaited Messiah.

THE REDEEMER

FOLLOWING Jesus

Jesus called his followers to be peacemakers. It takes courage and love to be a peacemaker. You can be a peacemaker by learning how to forgive others. When a person has hurt you, don't wait for an apology. Offer your hand in forgiveness before the person tells you he or she is sorry.

CHRIST WILL COME AGAIN

Jesus' resurrection was a remarkable event. Jesus had died but was now alive in a new way. His new life showed Jesus' friends what would happen to them when they died. It showed that God's reign was present on earth. But there is still more to tell. As you pray in the Creed, Jesus "ascended into heaven and is seated at the right hand of the Father. He will come again in glory to judge the living and the dead, and his kingdom will have no end."

THE REST OF THE STORY

Jesus left his followers two great commandments to live by: "You shall love the Lord, your God, with all your heart, with all your being, and with all your strength, and with all your mind, and your neighbor as yourself" (Luke 10:27). They would show their love for God and their neighbor in these ways:

- Bringing the message of God's love to the whole world.
- Working for peace and justice.
- Treating all people fairly and with respect.

Jesus said, "Whatever you do to your neighbor, you do to me. When you reach out to help others, it is Jesus you touch" (see Matthew 25:31–46).

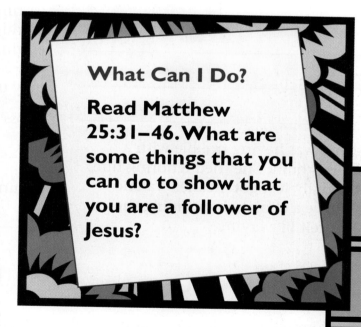

What Can I Do?

Read Matthew 25:31–46. What are some things that you can do to show that you are a follower of Jesus?

1. **What is the Paschal Mystery?**
2. **What are two ways that people honor the death of Jesus?**

37

DYING AND RISING

Jesus told his friends that following him would not always be easy. "Whoever wishes to come after me," he said, "must take up the cross and follow me" (*Matthew 16:24*).

Read about Ramón, Valerie, and Karla. In the space provided, tell what cross each is carrying. Then, tell how it can lead to resurrection.

Ramón was saving his paper route money for a trip with his friends to a big water park. Ramón's teacher asked the students to donate money to help a homeless family. Ramón felt sorry for this family, but he also wanted to go to the park with his friends.

Cross _____

_____

Resurrection _____

_____

Valerie was having trouble with a school-bus bully. She tried ignoring him, but the bully just got meaner. Valerie didn't have a choice about riding the bus. She felt like crying.

YOUR OWN CROSS

Jesus promised his followers that he would help them to carry their burdens. Think about a cross you are carrying. Use this prayer to ask Jesus for help.

Help me to follow you, Jesus, even when it is difficult. When I am wrong, help me to make things right. When I am hurt, help me to forgive. I praise you, Lord. Through the cross, you brought joy into the world. Alleluia!

WITH YOUR FAMILY

Go on an armchair pilgrimage. With someone in your family, read the Gospel of Luke, chapters 22–24. Divide it so that you read part of the Gospel each night of the week. By reflecting on the death and resurrection of Jesus, you can walk along with Jesus.

Cross _____

_____

Resurrection _____

_____

Karla wanted to be as cool as her older sister. Karla wore a pair of her sister's earrings to school without permission. During the day she lost one of the earrings. When Karla's sister found only one earring in her jewelry box, she was very upset.

Cross _____

_____

Resurrection _____

_____

▼ REVIEW CHAPTER 4 ....

CATHOLICS BELIEVE

1. Jesus suffered, died, and rose from the dead to save all people from sin and death.
2. Jesus' death, resurrection, and promised return is called the Paschal Mystery.

KNOW

Choose the correct word to complete the sentence.

1. Christians who travel to the Holy Land are known as (pilgrims, nomads, lifers).
2. Jesus suffered and died to save all people from (guilt, sin, suffering) and (fear, war, death).
3. Jesus' suffering, death, resurrection, and promised return are called the (Paschal, Passive, Pastoral) Mystery.
4. In the Creed, Catholics say that they believe Jesus "ascended into (space, heaven, air)."
5. You can be a pilgrim by making the (hour, union, stations) of the cross in your parish church.
6. Catholics believe that Jesus will come again to (judge, punish, finish) the living and the dead.

SUNDAY MASS

After the consecration, the deacon or priest says "Let us proclaim the mystery of our faith." The mystery proclaimed is the Paschal Mystery. The most common Memorial Acclamation used is "Christ has died, Christ is risen, Christ will come again."

CONTENT KEYS

1. **The Father is the first Person of the Trinity.**
2. **Jesus is the second Person of the Trinity.**
3. **The Holy Spirit is the third Person of the Trinity.**

I will ask, and the Father will give you another helper to be with you always, the Spirit of truth.

From JOHN 14:16

WHAT A RIDE!

You are on a roller coaster 200 feet in the air. You've just reached the top. In another instant you will raise your arms as the car you are in drops straight down.

Here you go!

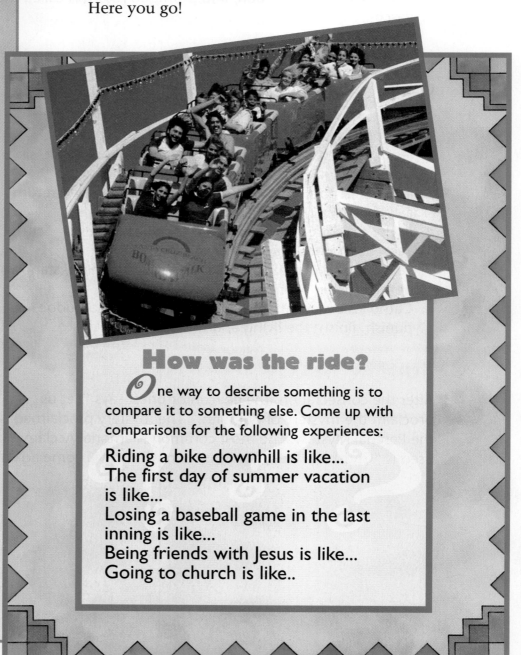

How was the ride?

One way to describe something is to compare it to something else. Come up with comparisons for the following experiences:

Riding a bike downhill is like...
The first day of summer vacation is like...
Losing a baseball game in the last inning is like...
Being friends with Jesus is like...
Going to church is like..

THE COMING OF THE HOLY SPIRIT

After a near-death experience, some people have said the experience was "like going through a tunnel toward a bright light." They used comparisons to describe an extraordinary experience. In the same way, the disciples of Jesus used comparisons to describe their experience of the Holy Spirit on Pentecost.

Ten days after Jesus returned to the Father, the Apostles, Mary, the Mother of Jesus, and many close friends of Jesus were together. They were sad because Jesus was gone. But they were also waiting and hopeful, because Jesus had promised to send them a Helper.

Suddenly the disciples knew that the Helper had come. No one knocked at the door or climbed through a window, but they knew that the Holy Spirit was present among them.

Later, when the Apostles wanted to describe the experience, they used comparisons. They said the Holy Spirit sounded like a strong, driving wind and appeared as tongues of fire over their heads.

Based on ACTS 2:1–4

What do you think the Apostles were trying to explain about their experience?

41

A POWERFUL HELPER

The evangelist John wrote his Gospel many years after the first Pentecost. John remembered the words of promise and comfort that Jesus spoke to his friends at the Last Supper. Jesus also used a comparison to describe the Holy Spirit. In John 14:16, Jesus calls the Holy Spirit an Advocate. An advocate is someone who speaks up for you, someone who takes your side. By calling the Holy Spirit the Advocate, Jesus was explaining that the Holy Spirit helps you stay close to God.

Gift of Life

Develop a symbol that shows the Holy Spirit as the giver of life.

THE GIVER OF LIFE

In many languages, the word *spirit* means "breath" or "wind"—the invisible power that makes things live and move. The Holy Spirit is like the wind. The coming of the Holy Spirit into your life is like having God give you mouth-to-mouth resuscitation. God's breath gives you new life, energy, and power.

In the Creed, you say the Holy Spirit is "the Lord, the Giver of Life, who proceeds from the Father and the Son." The Spirit is the gift of the Father and the Son to the world.

THE WORK OF THE SPIRIT

Like a strong wind blowing a sailboat across a lake, the Holy Spirit moved the disciples of Jesus. Whoosh! They were pushed from the room where they had been hiding. Whoosh! They began to tell everyone they saw about Jesus.

Like a strong wind, the Spirit carried the Good News quickly through the crowd. The Spirit helped the Apostles speak the right words so that people could understand and believe them. Belief in Jesus spread rapidly.

Later, the Holy Spirit continued working through the Church at Antioch (in Turkey), which sent Paul and Barnabas to preach about Jesus in other cities. As the first missionaries to Europe, they proclaimed their beliefs to strangers (see *Acts 13:2* and *16:11*).

The Holy Spirit continued to work in the Church after the Apostles died. The Holy Spirit is still at work wherever people follow Jesus.

Following Jesus

Fortitude means inner strength. Fortitude is also a virtue that helps you do what is right. The more you use your inner strength, the stronger it gets.

Think of one thing that is hard for you to do, such as doing your homework when you'd rather be playing a computer game. Each day this week, try to do the hard but right thing. As you learn to do small things, you develop the strength to do bigger ones.

THE FRUIT OF THE SPIRIT

Saint Paul compared the presence of the Spirit to the sight of ripe, juicy fruit on a healthy tree:

The fruit of the Spirit is love, joy, peace, patience, kindness, generosity, faithfulness, gentleness, self-control.

GALATIANS 5:22–23

When you see these qualities in people, you will know that the Holy Spirit is working in them—and getting results!

By Their Fruits

On each piece of fruit, write the name of a person and the good work he or she has produced. Use the fruit of the Spirit as a guide.

A FAMILY OF SAINTS

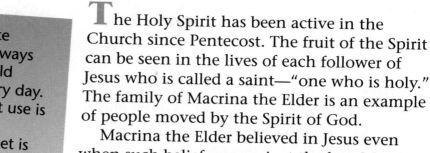

The Holy Spirit has been active in the Church since Pentecost. The fruit of the Spirit can be seen in the lives of each follower of Jesus who is called a saint—"one who is holy." The family of Macrina the Elder is an example of people moved by the Spirit of God.

Macrina the Elder believed in Jesus even when such belief was against the law. Macrina the Elder was tortured for her faith in Jesus, but she did not stop believing. Macrina passed along her strong faith to her children and grandchildren. Three of her grandchildren became famous saints.

At the age of twelve, Macrina the Younger dedicated her life to helping others in honor of God. Her brothers followed her example.

Basil became a priest and later a bishop. Basil became famous for his writings about the Holy Spirit. Because of his writing, he is known as Basil the Great!

Gregory also became a bishop. Gregory encouraged the followers of Jesus to practice justice. He even sold the property of his diocese to feed the poor.

Through Baptism, all Christians are called to be saints. Through the power and working of the Holy Spirit, ordinary people become holy. The Church, too, is a family of saints!

1. **Give one example of a fruit of the Spirit produced by Macrina's family.**
2. **People around you show the life of the Holy Spirit by their actions. Give one example of the Holy Spirit at work in the Church today.**

COME, HOLY SPIRIT!

Light a candle. Let the flame remind you that the Holy Spirit is present. Then pray with your class.

Leader: *Lord Jesus, you promised to send your Spirit to be with us always. Hear us as we pray:*

All: *Come, Holy Spirit! Fill the hearts of your faithful. And kindle in them the fire of your love.*

Leader: *Breathe new life into us, Holy Spirit. Make our love for you and for our brothers and sisters as strong and bright as fire.*

All: *Help us. Be with us. Speak for us when we do not know what to say. Be on our side against all evil. Teach us to see the truth.*

Leader: *Lord, we are your children, and we need you. Give us your life.*

All: *Send forth your Spirit, and they shall be created. And you will renew the face of the earth.*

WITH YOUR FAMILY

Ask your family to help you catch the Spirit "red-handed." Make a chart listing the fruit of the Spirit: love, joy, peace, patience, kindness, generosity, faithfulness, gentleness, and self-control. Hang the chart and a pencil on your refrigerator door. When someone recognizes the fruit of the Spirit in a family member, he or she should record it on the chart. At the end of one week, talk with your family about the results.

▼ REVIEW CHAPTER 5 · · · · · · · ·

CATHOLICS BELIEVE

1. The Father sent the Holy Spirit into the world to continue the work of Jesus.
2. With the Father and the Son, the Holy Spirit forms the Blessed Trinity.
3. The Holy Spirit is the Helper and Advocate Jesus promised to send.
4. The Holy Spirit came to the Church at Pentecost.

KNOW

Some important words about the Holy Spirit are hidden in this puzzle. Use the clues provided to help you identify the words. Then find the words and circle them.

Clues

Father, Son, and Holy Spirit _ _ _ _ _ _ _

A name for the Holy Spirit _ _ _ _ _ _ _ _

Another name for the Spirit _ _ _ _ _ _

The feast of the coming of
the Holy Spirit _ _ _ _ _ _ _ _ _

A fruit of the Holy Spirit _ _ _ _

Another fruit of the Spirit _ _ _ _ _

One who is holy _ _ _ _ _

One who is sent to carry
the Good News _ _ _ _ _ _ _ _ _ _

SUNDAY MASS

At the beginning of Eucharistic Prayer II, the priest prays: "Let your Spirit come upon these gifts to make them holy, so that they may become the body and blood of our Lord Jesus Christ." This is a sign that the Holy Spirit continues to work in the Church. Listen closely for this prayer at Mass this Sunday.

You have been called together in one Lord, one faith, one baptism, one God and Father of all.

From EPHESIANS 4:4–6

I WANT TO PLAY

Leslie stopped by the playground at Saint Monica's to watch the baseball team practice. She watched the coach hit fly balls to the eager players in the outfield. Shaking her head, Leslie turned and started to walk away. "I'd like to try out for the baseball team," she muttered to herself. "But they will never let me play."

"Hi!" the coach called out. "Do you want to play?"

Leslie couldn't believe her ears. "You mean you'd want me on your team?" Leslie managed to sputter.

"Why not? Everyone's welcome around here. I'm Coach Dixon. Grab a glove and hit the field."

Get In the Game

In the space provided, draw or write about a time when you were made to feel as if you belonged. How did you feel?

BROTHERS AND SISTERS

"**Y**ou come and tell us that Jesus says we are all brothers," the Tarascan leader told the priest. "You preach a God of love and peace, yet your people make slaves of us, rob us, and kill us."

The little Spanish priest nodded sadly. Everything that the Tarascan leader had said was true.

In 1519, Spanish soldiers conquered Mexico. They had come to the New World looking for gold and power. The governor and the soldiers forced the native people to work as slaves in the mines. They treated them as if they were less than human.

When the soldiers came, Spanish missionaries traveled with them. The missionaries came to bring the message of Jesus to the native people of Mexico. But the message was hard for the people to hear. The Spaniards' actions were so different from the words they spoke.

"If that is the kind of religion you bring us," the leader of the Tarascan people concluded, "we have no need of it."

SHOWING GOD'S LOVE

One Spanish official, Vasco de Quiroga, was saddened by how the native people were treated. He decided to make both his words and actions show people how much God loved them. At the age of sixty, Vasco de Quiroga became a priest and a bishop. He went to live among the Tarascan people.

Near Mexico City, Bishop de Quiroga established the first hospital in North America. He trained the native people to work as nurses. The hospital welcomed everyone who was sick or needy, Spaniard and Mexican alike. He founded the first school in which priests were taught the native languages of the Mexican people.

Because of the actions of this wise and loving bishop, many people learned that God loved them, too.

1. **Why did the Tarascan leader distrust the Spanish religion?**
2. **How did Vasco de Quiroga show by his actions that God loved all people?**
3. **What do you think Bishop Quiroga accomplished by treating the Tarascans with respect?**

WHAT WOULD YOU DO ?

Draw an action that shows God's love.

THE CHURCH CALLS PEOPLE TOGETHER

The Church is made up of many people who come together as one in a community. In the Bible, the Church is called the People of God, the Body of Christ, a vine with branches, and a sheepfold with gates open to all the sheep.

When you came into the Catholic Church, you answered an invitation from the Holy Spirit. You may have entered the Church as an infant or as a young child. If you were baptized as an infant or young child, your parents and godparents accepted the invitation for you. Other people receive the Spirit's invitation as older children or adults. Whenever people enter the Church, they are saying "yes" to the Spirit's invitation.

WE'RE GLAD YOU'RE HERE

In the space provided, show how new members are welcomed into your parish community. Are new parishioners introduced at Mass? Does the parish have a welcoming committee? If you don't know, how would you find out?

THE CHURCH'S MISSION

Jesus established the Church for a purpose. He wanted his followers to stick together. He called them to grow strong in love for one another as he loved them. He sent them to spread the Good News of salvation to every nation. He told them to be faithful to everything he had taught them. This is the mission of the Church.

The mission of the Church is to be one, holy, catholic, and apostolic. These qualities, found in the Nicene Creed, are called the **marks of the Church.** The Church can be recognized by how it lives these marks.

Jesus sent the Holy Spirit to work in and with the members of the Church. The marks of the Church describe what the Holy Spirit is doing in the Church. They also describe what the Holy Spirit is doing in you and what you should do as a Catholic.

- **The Church is one.** The Holy Spirit joins believers together in Christ. Catholics are one because they are united in following Jesus. They share one Baptism and one leader, the pope.
- **The Church is holy.** The Holy Spirit lives in the hearts of Christ's followers. Catholics are holy because they work with the Holy Spirit to bring God's love, mercy, peace, and justice to the world.

- **The Church is catholic.** Catholic means "universal," or "open to all." The Holy Spirit invites all people to the Church. Catholics accept and welcome anyone who wants to follow Jesus.
- **The Church is apostolic.** The Holy Spirit guides the teaching of the Church through the successors of the Apostles. Missionaries pass on the Gospel message taught by the Apostles.

Including other people is one way to follow Jesus. When you include people who may feel left out in your groups and in your games, you build up good feelings and form new friendships.

IS THIS ALL THERE IS?

At the end of the Creed, the Church prays: "We look for the resurrection of the dead, and the life of the world to come." Those who have lived in the Spirit will live forever in God's kingdom.

The Church is a sign that God's kingdom has begun. Followers of Jesus build God's kingdom of love by welcoming others, by being teachers and missionaries, by forgiving one another, by respecting others, and by living in a way that invites others to follow Jesus.

The Holy Spirit calls people to this work all the time.

1. **In your own words, explain what the Church is trying to do.**
2. **Provide examples of the four marks of the Church from the work of Bishop Vasco de Quiroga.**
3. **Give two examples of ways people in your parish are signs of God's kingdom.**

It's Your Church

How well do you know your Catholic community? Gather information for each of the statements that follow. Work with your teacher and classmates to learn more.

Name of my parish

Name of my diocese

Name of my bishop

Name of my pastor

Others who work in my parish

One way my parish welcomes people

One way my parish reaches out to others

YOU ARE SENT

You are called to be a missionary. You do not have to travel to distant lands or learn new languages. You can share the Good News right now. Use these questions to help you decide where to begin.

WITH YOUR FAMILY

Ask members of your family what they like best about being Catholic. Try to find one practical way your family can share what it likes best with people who are not Catholic.

1. Who needs to hear the Good News?

2. What Good News do I have to share?

3. How will I share the Good News?

Stand while your teacher prays for your success.

Teacher: *Holy Spirit, send out these young people to teach as Jesus did. Help them to teach by what they say, and also by what they do. Give them the courage to reach out to others. Give them the strength to do what they know is right. Give them plenty of joy and peace to share. We ask this in the name of the Father, and of the Son, and of the Holy Spirit.*

All: *Amen.*

CATHOLICS BELIEVE

1. The Church is the People of God, called together by the Holy Spirit.
2. The Church is one, holy, catholic, and apostolic.
3. The Church is on a mission to serve the whole world.

KNOW

Solve the clues and write the correct term on each line. When you are finished, read the boxed letters from top to bottom. You should find an important word from this chapter.

Clues

1. This word means *universal*.
2. The Spirit lives in the Church to make it _____.
3. The Catholic Church is a _____ of people called together by the Holy Spirit.
4. Catholics believe in the _____ of the dead.
5. This mark means the Church carries on the message of the Apostles.
6. Jesus sent his followers to _____ the whole world.

         1. (_) _ _ _ _ _ _ _
         2. (_) _ _ _
      3. _ _ _ _ _ (_) _ _ _ _
     4. _ _ _ _ _ _ (_) _ _ _ _ _ _
  5. _ _ _ _ _ _ _ _ _ (_)
      6. _ _ _ _ _ (_)

SUNDAY MASS

The General Intercessions, prayed after the Creed at Mass, are prayers for the needs of the Church. There are prayers for the leaders of the Church, the Church in the whole world, and the Church in your own parish. This Sunday, listen carefully to each intercession. Be sure to respond, "Lord, hear our prayer" or the response used in your parish.

CELEBRATING MARY'S FEAST DAYS

Catholics celebrate six major feast days during the year in honor of Jesus' mother, Mary. These days remember important times in Mary's life. When you celebrate these feast days, you learn what it means to follow Jesus.

◆ **SEPTEMBER 8**

Feast of the Nativity of Mary

In many parts of the world, the birthday of Mary is celebrated as a harvest festival. The finest grapes and wheat are presented before Mary's statue and then shared with the poor.

◆ **DECEMBER 8**

Feast of the Immaculate Conception

Mary was free of sin from the very first moment of her life.

◆ **DECEMBER 12**

Feast of Our Lady of Guadaloupe

Mary is the patroness of the Americas. Dancers in native dress perform outside the Basilica of Our Lady of Guadaloupe in Mexico.

◆ **JANUARY 1**

Feast of Mary, Mother of God

Mary is honored as the mother of Jesus and the Mother of the Church.

◆ MARCH 25
Feast of the Annunciation

Mary received the Good News that she was to be the Mother of the Savior. For many centuries in Europe, this feast was celebrated as New Year's Day.

◆ AUGUST 15
Feast of the Assumption

At the end of her life, Mary was taken body and soul to be with her son in heaven. In many parts of the world, the flowers, fruit, and medicinal herbs grown in summer are blessed on this day. In New England, Portuguese Catholics celebrate this day by blessing their fishing boats.

◆ MAY

The entire month of May is dedicated to Mary. Catholics celebrate during the month of May with processions in Mary's honor and the crowning of Mary's statue with a garland of flowers.

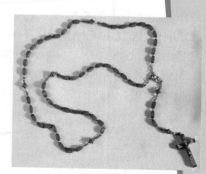

◆ OCTOBER

October is the month of the Rosary, Mary's special prayer.

◆ TODAY

Plan a celebration to honor Mary. Use a picture or statue of Mary, or make a banner. Decorate the room with flowers. March around the room in a procession, carrying a statue of Mary raised in the air. Sing and pray hymns in honor of Mary.

UNIT 1 REVIEW

LEARNING

1. **What is the Blessed Trinity?** The Blessed Trinity is the One God, who is Father, Son, and Holy Spirit.
2. **Why do we say that God is the Creator?** God made the world and breathed life into every human being. God continues to care for all creation.
3. **Who is Jesus?** Jesus Christ is true God and true man. He is the Son of God and the Savior of the world.
4. **How did Jesus save us from sin and death?** Jesus suffered, died, and rose from the dead to save us from sin and death. Jesus will come again.
5. **Who is the Holy Spirit?** The Holy Spirit is the gift of the Father and the Son. With the Father and the Son, the Holy Spirit forms the Blessed Trinity.
6. **What is the Church?** The Church is the People of God, called together by the Holy Spirit. The Church is one, holy, catholic, and apostolic.

PRAYING

All: We believe in Jesus Christ!

1: Though he was in the form of God, he did not insist on being equal to God.
2: Rather, he emptied himself, taking our own human form.
3: He humbled himself, becoming obedient to death, even death on a cross.
4: Because of this, God raised him up, and gave him the name that is above all others in heaven and on earth.

All: We believe that Jesus Christ is Lord, with the Holy Spirit, to the glory of God the Father!

ASKING

1. What new thing have I learned about my Catholic faith?
2. How do I show in my life that I believe in God?

LIVING

Fill in the survey below. When you have finished the survey, compare answers with a partner.

Write in your answer	Write yes or no
My hair color	All people are my brothers and sisters.
My month of birth	All people should be treated with love.
My favorite hobby	I want to help the hungry or homeless.

I Belong

Together you are one body in Christ.

God sent Jesus so that the works of God might be made visible through him.

From JOHN 9:3

A POWERFUL LIGHT

Betsy and Carmen raced up the last few steps to the top of Rocky Point lighthouse. The girls gazed spellbound across the ocean toward the islands off the coast of Maine.

"So what do you think?" asked Betsy.

"Cool!" Carmen whispered in awe.

"Phew!" gasped Carmen's dad, finally catching up. "I must have climbed 200 steps."

"Stop here," he read the sign aloud. "Gladly," he said with a final gasp.

"Look at the size of that mirror," said Betsy, pointing to the huge beacon at the top of the lighthouse. "The sign says that the mirror is designed to magnify the light of the bulb thousands of times so sailors can see it from miles away."

"Awesome," Carmen answered. "I'd like to stay here forever," she said, gazing at the breathtaking view from the window.

"The lady in the shop said they're expecting a heavy storm, a real northeaster," her dad informed them. "We can't stay long."

"I guess storms are one reason there are lighthouses," Betsy replied.

"Hey, where did the islands go?" asked Carmen.

"The islands have been covered by storm clouds," said Carmen's dad. "They sure are moving fast. Maybe we should take that as a sign to head back to the motel."

"Right!" agreed Betsy, giving Carmen a high five. "Let's get out of here!"

1. **What do you learn from each of these signs in the story: sign at top of lighthouse steps, mirror at top of lighthouse, clouds covering islands, high five sign?**
2. **What are some other common signs? What do these signs tell you?**

SIGN IN, PLEASE

DRAW A SIGN THAT INDICATES HOW YOU FEEL RIGHT NOW. ASK YOUR CLASSMATES TO TELL WHAT YOUR SIGN MEANS.

SIGNS OF FAITH

People communicate through signs all the time. Some signs are things, like a stop sign. Other signs are words, like "Wow." Still other signs are actions, like hugging your parents. Christians use signs to show the world what they believe and how they follow Jesus.

The cross was a sign of shameful death in Jesus' time. It became a sign of hope to Jesus' followers after his resurrection.

In the Middle Ages, Christian knights and kings wore the cross on their armor. They were called Crusaders, which means "cross bearers."

Today you wear a cross as a proud sign that you follow Jesus.

Loaves and fish are used in this early Christian mosaic as a sign of how Jesus fed his followers (John 6:1–13). Loaves and fish are signs of the Eucharist, too. Jesus continues to feed his followers in the Eucharist.

Alpha and omega are the first and last letters of the Greek alphabet. These letters are a sign that Jesus is the beginning and the end of everything. He always was and always will be (Revelation 1:8, 21:6).

The chi-rho is a monogram for Jesus. It combines the first two Greek letters of the title Christ.

1. **What are Catholics saying when they make the sign of the cross?**
2. **Name three signs of faith that you have seen in your classroom or in your parish church.**

A Sign from God

I used to see an old man sitting by the roadside begging. He would hold out his hand and call, "Help a poor blind man!" Sometimes people would stop and give him a coin.

One hot day a crowd of people came down the road. As usual, the beggar called out to them. Someone in the group asked, "Rabbi, was it this man's sin or that of his parents that caused him to be born blind?"

The rabbi reached out and took the blind beggar's hand. Then he said, "Neither he nor his parents sinned; this man is blind so that the goodness and power of God can be shown through him." What could he mean by that? I wondered. But the rabbi didn't explain. Well, at least not in words.

I watched everything the rabbi did. First he crouched down at the man's side

and spit on the ground. Then he used his fingers to make mud. Then I heard him say in a quiet voice, "I am the light of the world." Finally he touched the man's eyes gently and rubbed mud over them. This rabbi was sure different from the ones I knew.

The rabbi told the blind man to wash off the mud in the pool of Siloam. The old man did exactly what the rabbi said, without asking even one question. I was still curious, so I followed him. He obviously went to the pool often because he had no trouble finding his way there. When we reached the pool, I stood back and watched as he washed off the mud.

SEEING IS BELIEVING

Before my very eyes I saw a miracle happen. As soon as the water washed away the mud, the old man could see! He shouted. He laughed. He rubbed his eyes and looked around in amazement. Suddenly the man started to sing the praises of God.

The rabbi returned a little later. He went up to the beggar and asked, "Do you believe in the **Son of Man**?" The beggar answered, "Who is the Son of Man, that I may believe in him?" The rabbi smiled and said, "You see him standing before you."

"I do believe, Lord," the man said, falling to his knees.

I saw it happen. I believe, too.

Based on JOHN 9:1–7

1. **What signs did Jesus use to cure the blind man?**
2. **What was communicated by each of the signs?**

SIGNS AND WONDERS

Jesus used many signs. Look up each of these Scripture readings. Tell what sign Jesus used. Then tell what you think the sign means.

Scripture	Sign	What the Sign Means
Matthew 15:32–39		
Luke 5:17–26		
Luke 7:11–15		

Jesus Is a Sign

Jesus used signs—mud, touch, words, and water—when he cured the blind man. He could just as easily have said to the man, "See," and the man would have seen. Instead, Jesus took ordinary things and filled them to overflow with God's love.

Jesus didn't just use signs to heal people. He himself is also a sign. In Jesus you see the Father *(John 14:9),* you feel God's love, and you receive God's gift of eternal life.

Jesus said that he was the Light of the World. Just as a lighthouse provides a sign of hope to ships caught at sea in a storm, Jesus provides a sign of hope for people looking for help throughout their lives.

The Church Is a Sign

The Church is a sign, too. Whoever sees the Church sees Jesus. Every member of the Church is a sign that Jesus lived, died, and rose from the dead. When the Church does the things that Jesus did or teaches what Jesus taught, it is a sign of Christ. Jesus continues to act in the Church through the sacraments. They are grace-filled signs of Christ.

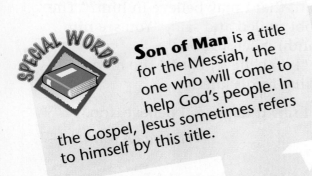

SPECIAL WORDS

Son of Man is a title for the Messiah, the one who will come to help God's people. In the Gospel, Jesus sometimes refers to himself by this title.

FOLLOWING Jesus

Your actions and words are signs. You may not think you are a leader, but younger children and your own classmates see what you do. When you do what is good and right, some others will follow your good example. Setting a good example is one way that you can follow Jesus. Set a good example every day for a week. Keep track of how it is catching on.

SACRAMENTS ARE SIGNS

The Church continues to do what Jesus did in the seven signs known as sacraments. Like Jesus, the Church uses ordinary objects, actions, and words in the sacraments to show what God is doing. In the sacraments, the invisible God speaks, acts, nourishes, and heals people through the signs of bread, wine, oil, rings, water, and touch. The sacraments bring God's strength and life, healing and love into your life.

SACRAMENT	NAME	SIGNS
Sacraments of initiation	**Baptism**	Water, oil, sign of the cross, white garment, lit candle
	Confirmation	Oil, sign of the cross, handshake
	Eucharist	Bread, wine
Sacraments of healing	**Reconciliation** (Penance)	Confession of sins, sign of the cross, absolution
	Anointing of the sick	Oil, sign of the cross, laying on of hands
Sacraments of vocation	**Marriage**	Couple, rings
	Holy Orders	Oil, laying on of hands

DID YOU KNOW?

Sacramentals are objects that help Catholics remember God's presence. Sacramentals such as holy water, blessed ashes, palm branches, incense, and candles are used in community prayer and celebration.

When the Church celebrates the sacraments, the members of the Church receive new life, nourishment, healing, strength, and forgiveness. These graces come through the life-giving power of the passion, death, and resurrection of Jesus. Grace is a sharing in God's own life and friendship. For this reason, the sacraments are really more than signs. In the sacraments, you actually meet God. You share in God's life and God's love.

1. **Which sacraments have you celebrated?**
2. **Explain how the sacraments you have celebrated are signs of God's love.**

SIGN OF THE CROSS

When people enter the catechumenate, they are signed with the cross in a special ceremony. The signing calls down God's blessing to make them strong enough to follow Jesus.

This prayer is taken from that ceremony. Choose a partner. Stand facing each other. Take turns doing what the leader says. What do you learn from these signs?

Leader: *I trace the sign of the cross on your forehead and ask Jesus to strengthen you with this sign of his love.*

Response: *Praise to you, Lord Jesus Christ.*

Leader: *I trace the sign of the cross on your ears and ask Jesus to help you hear his voice.*

Response: *Praise to you, Lord Jesus Christ.*

Leader: *I trace the sign of the cross on your hands and pray that others will see Jesus in all the work you do.*

Response: *Praise to you, Lord Jesus Christ.*

Leader: *I trace the sign of the cross on your eyes and ask Jesus to help you see him in other people.*

Response: *Praise to you, Lord Jesus Christ.*

Leader: *I trace the sign of the cross on your shoulders and ask Jesus to help you carry your cross.*

Response: *Praise to you, Lord Jesus Christ.*

Leader: *I trace the sign of the cross on your feet and ask Jesus to help you always walk with him.*

Response: *Praise to you, Lord Jesus Christ.*

Look for signs of Catholic identity in your home. List these signs. Talk with your parents to see why these signs were chosen for your home.

▼ REVIEW CHAPTER 7

CATHOLICS BELIEVE

1. Sacraments are signs and celebrations of God's power and love.
2. Through the sacraments, Catholics share in God's life of grace.

KNOW

Complete each sentence by choosing the right word from the parentheses.

1. Jesus used (mud, wine) as a sign when he cured the blind man.
2. Jesus is a sign of the (Father, pope).
3. The Church has seven special signs called (sanctuaries, sacraments).
4. Holy water, ashes, and palm branches are examples of (sacramentals, sanctifiers).
5. The *ichthus* is a Christian sign shaped like a (loaf of bread, fish).
6. Through the sacraments, members of the Church share in the (devotion, grace) of God.
7. Jesus used signs to show God's (creation, love).

SUNDAY MASS

Almost everything the priest and people do during the Mass is a sign of what they believe and a sign that Jesus is present among them. This week when you sit and stand, pray and sing at Mass, think about what all of the signs are saying. When you participate in the actions of the liturgy, you are praying as part of the community.

A New Birth

Content Keys

1. Baptism is the first sacrament of the Church.
2. Baptism initiates a person into the Church.
3. Baptism calls you to a life of loving service.

Jesus saved us through the water of rebirth and renewal by the Holy Spirit.

TITUS 3:5

Water Makes Me Free

"Evie Vitutis is a remarkable girl," said her coach after the meet. "She is a strong swimmer and a real team player."

A fifth-grader at Saint Elizabeth's School, Evie swims with the Flying Fins Swim Club. On Saturday she anchored the Flying Fins relay team as they deep-sixed the Sea Creatures, 85 to 75.

What makes Evie's triumph so remarkable is that she has juvenile arthritis and can barely walk. On land she must use a wheelchair to get around. Walking is just too painful. But in water she is like a dolphin—fast, smooth, and sleek. The buoyancy of the water allows Evie to move without hurting.

"The water makes me free," says Evie, beaming. "I can move just as I want. Nothing holds me back. When I'm in the water, I feel like a whole new me!"

Catch the Wave

What water activities do you enjoy? Discuss your favorite water activity with a friend.

WATER AND SPIRIT

Nicodemus was puzzled. He kept God's laws faithfully. He prayed at the Temple, where he was one of the leaders. He had waited and waited for God's kingdom to come. Nicodemus was surprised to hear Jesus claim that the kingdom could be seen around him. Nicodemus was determined to ask Jesus for an explanation.

Nicodemus did not want anyone to see him visit Jesus, so he chose a very dark night to make his trip. He slipped silently down a back street to the place where Jesus was staying. He and Jesus met on the rooftop in darkness. During their conversation, Nicodemus asked Jesus about God's kingdom.

"Rabbi," Nicodemus began, "I know that you have come from God, for no one can do the signs that you are doing unless God is with him."

Jesus answered, "No one can see the kingdom of God without being born again from above."

BEING BORN AGAIN

Nicodemus was stunned. This was the strangest thing he had ever heard! "How can a person once grown old be born again?" he said. "Surely he cannot go back into his mother's womb and be born a second time."

Nicodemus was glad it was dark. He felt embarrassed that he did not understand what Jesus meant. He could feel his cheeks turning red under his beard.

But Jesus did not think Nicodemus was foolish. Jesus was very patient. He tried again to explain. "A person must be born of water and spirit in order to enter into the kingdom of God."

Jesus and Nicodemus talked long into the night. Nicodemus did not understand everything Jesus said, but he knew he was hearing the truth. He knew God's kingdom was very near.

Based on JOHN 3:1–7

1. **What does it mean to be born again?**
2. **What problems did Nicodemus have accepting what Jesus said?**

You get new ideas every day—from friends, from movies, from books and magazines, from parents and teachers, and from the radio and TV. Some of these ideas are good, and others are not. How do you know which is which? To choose between ideas, you need to learn how to evaluate them. Use these steps to judge whether an idea is good.

1. Ask the Holy Spirit for the gift of understanding.
2. Ask yourself, "Will this help or hurt others? What will it do to me?"
3. Find out what Jesus said about it.
4. Find out what the Church says about it.
5. Ask a parent or trusted adult for advice.

Evaluating new ideas in this way will help you live and grow as a follower of Jesus.

Join In •

If you were sitting on the roof with Jesus and Nicodemus, what questions would you ask Jesus about being born again?

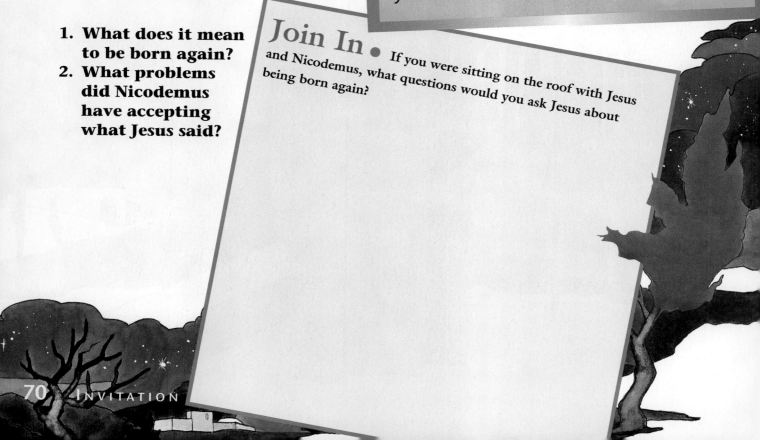

NEW LIFE

Your birth was a special event. It can never be repeated. But you can change your attitude and behavior at any time. You may not have changed physically, but you can change who you are. It's almost like becoming a new person.

Jesus told Nicodemus that Baptism—being born of water and spirit—was like being born again. When people are baptized, they are changed and are "born again" into God's family. Through God's grace, they are newly created and with Jesus can truly call God "father." Once you are a child of God through grace, you remain that way. Just as you are only born once, you need only to be baptized once. Baptism marks you forever as God's child.

SACRAMENT OF INITIATION

On the day you were born, you were welcomed into the human family. On the day you were baptized, you were welcomed into God's family and became a child of God. You began your new life as a follower of Jesus on that day.

As a child of God, you are part of God's family and a member of the Church. Everyone who shares in the new life of Baptism is your brother or sister. You have a big family you can count on to support and guide you.

Through the sacrament of Baptism, the Catholic community welcomed you as a new member. The community has helped you to grow in the faith. From the community, you have learned to live as a follower of Jesus. That is why Baptism is called a **sacrament of initiation.** In Baptism, you were welcomed into the Body of Christ and introduced into the belief and practices of the Church.

SPECIAL WORDS

Baptism, Confirmation, and Eucharist are the **sacraments of initiation.** These three sacraments welcome people into the Church.

THE SIGN OF WATER

Water is very important to human life. Your body is mostly water. You drink water when you are thirsty. You cook food in water. You play in water. Water can also be very dangerous. You can drown in water. During floods, water can uproot trees and destroy buildings.

Because of its life-giving and destructive power, water is a powerful sign. That is why water is the main sign of Baptism. Going down into the water of Baptism is a sign of dying with Jesus. Coming up again from the water is a sign of rising with Jesus. In Baptism you became a Christian by sharing in the death and resurrection of Jesus.

Water is also used for cleaning. Just as water washes away dirt from your body and clothes, water in Baptism washes away sin. Baptism cleanses you of both original sin and personal sins. Baptism wipes away all of those selfish actions and choices that separated you from God. In the water of Baptism, you were refreshed and recreated by the spirit, grace, and love of God. You are ready to begin a new friendship with God.

DID YOU KNOW?

Anyone may baptize a person who is in danger of death and who requests Baptism. To baptize someone, pour ordinary water on the person's head while saying, "I baptize you in the name of the Father, and of the Son, and of the Holy Spirit."

OTHER SIGNS OF BAPTISM

Besides water, there are several other signs of Baptism.

- Baptism by immersion—going all the way under the water and then stepping out again—is a full sign of the death and resurrection of Jesus.
- The words "I baptize you in the name of the Father, and of the Son, and of the Holy Spirit" are a sign that God in the Trinity is present.
- The white garment worn by the newly baptized person is another sign of new life and cleanliness.
- The baptismal candle is lit from the Paschal candle. It is a sign that the light of Christ now shines in the baptized person.

LIVING THE NEW LIFE

Baptism marks the beginning of your new life in Christ. Think of two ways that you can show Christ's love for the following people:

► A classmate who was not chosen to play on a team during lunch

► Someone who has taken your favorite pencil

► Younger brothers and sisters who annoy you

► Poor people begging for food

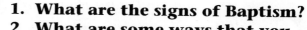

1. **What are the signs of Baptism?**
2. **What are some ways that you have been initiated into the Catholic community?**

CELEBRATE NEW LIFE

Pray this prayer together as a class.

Reader 1: *A reading from the first letter of John. "God sent Jesus into the world so that we might have life through him. If God so loved us, we must also love one another. No one has ever seen God. Yet if we love one another, God remains in us. This is how we know God has given us the Spirit."*

From 1 JOHN 4:9, 12–13

This is the Word of the Lord.

All: *Blessed be God who gives us new life!*

Reader 2: *Father, through the water of Baptism you filled us with new life as your very own children.*

All: *Blessed be God who gives us new life!*

Reader 3: *You set us free and filled our hearts with the Spirit of your love.*

All: *Blessed be God who gives us new life!*

Reader 4: *You call us to live our new life every day by showing love for others.*

All: *Blessed be God who gives us new life!*

(Dipping your hand in water, make the sign of the cross, praying)

All: *In the name of the Father, and of the Son, and of the Holy Spirit. Amen.*

WITH YOUR FAMILY

Just as you celebrate the day that you were born with a party, you can celebrate the day of your new birth in Baptism. Find out from your parents when you were baptized. Look at photos and mementos with your family. Plan to celebrate the anniversary of your baptism.

▼ REVIEW CHAPTER 8

CATHOLICS BELIEVE

1. The sacrament of Baptism gives people new life, frees them from sin, and makes them members of the Catholic community.
2. Baptism is one of the sacraments of initiation.

KNOW

Carefully read each of the statements below. Choose **T** if the statement is true. Choose **F** if the statement is false.

(T) F **1.** In Baptism, the pouring of water is a sign of new life in the Holy Spirit.

T (F) **2.** Nicodemus was not interested in learning about the kingdom of God.

(T) F **3.** Jesus said that people should be born again of water and the spirit.

(T) F **4.** Christians are baptized in the name of the Father and of the Son, and of the Holy Spirit.

(T) F **5.** Baptism washes away original sin.

T (F) **6.** Christians should be baptized when they are born and again before they die.

(T) F **7.** Baptism makes a person part of the Christian community.

SUNDAY MASS

When Catholics gather to celebrate the Sunday Eucharist, they usually bless themselves with holy water before entering the church. This is a sign that they are renewing their baptism. This Sunday, renew your baptism when you enter the church. Dip the fingers of your right hand into the holy water font. Then carefully sign yourself with the cross and say, "In the name of the Father, and of the Son, and of the Holy Spirit. Amen."

SEALED WITH THE HOLY SPIRIT

1. Confirmation completes Baptism.
2. The Holy Spirit enables Christians to follow Jesus.
3. Confirmation is one of the three sacraments of initiation.

You will receive the gift of the Holy Spirit.

ACTS 2:38

STRONG IN THE SPIRIT

Boniface held his breath. What he was about to do was very difficult and very dangerous. But unless he acted, his mission would fail. Boniface was frightened, but he was also very brave. As long as the Hessians worshiped this tree, they would never accept Jesus as Lord. He knew that God was with him. He knew that he would succeed with God's help. He grasped the ax firmly, whispered a prayer, and then stepped forward.

The crowd of Hessians murmured in fear and wonder at this brave man. This place, on Mount Gudenberg, was sacred to their god, Donar. Donar himself, they believed, lived in the great oak that Boniface, the Christian bishop, was about to chop down. Surely, the Hessians thought, lightning would strike him dead.

Boniface did not hesitate. Swinging the heavy ax, he cried out, "The Spirit of God is with me!" The mighty blow landed with a thunderous crack. Instantly the mighty tree split into four pieces.

Boniface looked at the damage his one swing had caused and smiled. The idol had been destroyed. Boniface was always amazed by what he could accomplish through the Spirit of God.

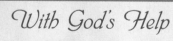

With God's Help

Describe a time when you were afraid. What helped you overcome your fears?

THE SPIRIT OF GOD IS WITH ME

Saint Boniface was a man of action. He had been sent by the pope from England to Germany to preach the Good News to the German tribes. With God's help, Boniface was very successful in his work.

- With the wood of the oak tree, Boniface built a church on the summit of Mount Gudenberg.
  - He made friends of the German tribes that had considered him an enemy.
  - He brought Jesus' message of peace to people who worshiped the god of war.

Boniface did not work alone. He was helped by other English monks and nuns. The monasteries they built throughout the country became centers of civilization. The monks and nuns started schools and passed along better farming methods. Their monasteries provided safe housing for travelers. They nursed the sick and fed the hungry.

When the people saw the good things the followers of Jesus did, they were impressed. Many people became Christians. By the time of his death, Boniface had baptized and confirmed thousands of people from the German tribes. With an inner strength that came from the Holy Spirit, he accomplished great things. Boniface is called the Apostle to the Germans.

DID YOU KNOW?

Saint Boniface was named Winfrid when he was baptized. When Winfrid was almost forty years old, Pope Gregory II sent him to do missionary work in Germany. To honor this brave missionary, the pope gave Winfrid the new name of Boniface, which in Latin means "doer of good things."

In many cultures, people are given new names at important times of their lives. At Confirmation, people choose a new name to show that they are celebrating an important life event.

The Spirit at Work

Boniface and the other missionaries who worked with him accomplished great things, but they did not act alone. Each of them had received the Holy Spirit at Baptism. They had been sealed by the gifts of the Spirit in Confirmation. With the Holy Spirit's help, there was no end to the good they could accomplish.

At Baptism, you were anointed with oil and given your name in Christ. At Confirmation, you will be marked with the seal of the Holy Spirit and receive the Spirit's seven gifts.

Wisdom: helps you see God, yourself, and others as God sees you.

Understanding: helps you to see the truth in your relationship with God, with others, and with yourself.

Right judgment: helps you to make good decisions and act on your beliefs.

Courage: helps you to act on your beliefs, to use your God-given talents bravely, and to reach out to others in loving service.

Knowledge: helps you to know and be known by God, yourself, and others in a deeper way.

Reverence: moves you to show respect for God and for all the people and things God made.

Wonder and awe: help you to remain open to the surprising, delightful, loving presence of God in your life and to respond to God with goodness and love.

1. **What are the seven gifts of the Holy Spirit?**
2. **What was Saint Boniface able to accomplish because he used the Spirit's gifts?**

Useful Gifts

You can see the gifts of the Holy Spirit in the good works done by Saint Boniface and the other missionaries. Using the space provided, tell a story about how you have used one or more of the gifts of the Spirit. Be prepared to read your story to the class.

ANOINTED IN CHRIST

When a person is confirmed, the bishop anoints the person's forehead with chrism, a perfumed olive oil that is blessed and used in the sacraments of Baptism, Confirmation, and Holy Orders. Laying his hands on the person's head, the bishop prays, "Be sealed with the gift of the Holy Spirit."

A seal is a symbol of a person's authority or ownership. Often the seal was a design carved on a ring. The ring was pressed into hot wax to leave an imprint. The seal indicated that what was in the letter came from the ring's owner. If the seal was broken, the letter was then questionable. The seal of the Holy Spirit marks the Christian as belonging to Christ forever. The gift of the Holy Spirit received in Baptism is confirmed and strengthened in Confirmation.

Saint Boniface understood the importance of a seal. After being made a bishop, Boniface returned to his work in Germany. Pope Gregory II sent along a sealed letter to Charles Martel, the powerful ruler of the Franks. Martel read the letter and recognized the authority of the pope.

Martel gave Boniface another document that announced to the German tribes that Boniface and his companions were protected by the king. He placed his official seal upon it so that everyone would know that this document came from him.

Thanks to these two documents, Boniface's missionary work went well.

In much the same way, the seal of Confirmation is a valuable gift for Christians. The Christian is sealed or marked with the Spirit of God. Just as the seal of Charles Martel identified Boniface as a friend of the king, so the seal of the Holy Spirit marks a Christian as a follower of Christ. The seal of confirmation is a sign that the Holy Spirit is present, offering support, encouragement, strength, and protection.

THE SIGN OF OIL

In biblical times, oil pressed from olives was a sign of abundance and joy. When the crop was good and the oil was plentiful, the people celebrated a festival. Oil was used to prepare food, cleanse and perfume the body, and dress the hair. Oil was a sign of prosperity and strength.

In ancient times, oil was used to heal wounds and strengthen the body. Athletes rubbed oil on their muscles to warm up for competition. Oil is still used today in ointments and soothing lotions. In Confirmation, the anointing with oil suggests the strength and readiness that comes from the presence of the Holy Spirit.

Oil was also used to anoint kings. It marked them as belonging to or chosen by God. The sweet-smelling chrism of Confirmation is used as a sign of a Christian's willingness to serve others in the kingdom of God.

LAYING ON OF HANDS

In ancient Jewish custom, laying on of hands was the way of choosing a person for a task and asking God's blessing and power to carry it out. The laying on of hands in Confirmation goes back to the time of the Apostles.

When the Apostles in Jerusalem heard that the people of Samaria had accepted the word of God, they sent Peter and John, who went down and prayed for them, that they might receive the Holy Spirit, for it had not yet fallen upon any of them; they had only been baptized in the name of the Lord Jesus. Then the Apostles laid hands on them and they received the Holy Spirit.

ACTS 8:14–17

BAPTISM AND CONFIRMATION

There is no set age for Confirmation. Some Christians are confirmed immediately after Baptism, some are confirmed in second grade, others are confirmed in eighth grade, and still others in high school.

Children baptized after infancy are often confirmed at their baptism. This is done because Confirmation was originally part of Baptism. Remember Gallia? When she and her family were initiated into the Church at the Easter Vigil, they received the sacrament of Confirmation immediately after they were baptized.

Over time, Confirmation practices changed. As the number of Christians increased, it became impossible for a bishop to be present at all baptisms. The anointing with chrism by the bishop became a separate ceremony. With the laying on of hands and the words, "Be sealed with the gift of the Holy Spirit," this anointing forms the sacrament of Confirmation.

When adults and older children join the Church today, they celebrate Baptism, Confirmation, and Eucharist at the same Mass.

1. **What are the signs of Confirmation?**
2. **What are some of the traditional uses for oil?**
3. **Explain the reasons for using oil in the sacrament of Confirmation.**
4. **Explain how Baptism and Confirmation are related.**

Signed, Sealed, Delivered

Design your own seal to show that you belong to Christ and to the Church. Share your design with your classmates and family.

FOLLOWING Jesus

Saint Boniface was a bold, courageous man. He tackled big challenges. But it takes courage to deal with little challenges, too. It takes courage to tell the truth, to do your homework instead of watching TV, or to say "no" when a friend dares you to do something wrong, like spray paint the neighbor's fence. Use the Holy Spirit's gift of courage today. Write an act of courage that you have done next to your seal to show that this is one way you choose to follow Jesus.

YOU BELONG TO CHRIST

The sacraments of initiation make you a member of the Church, the Body of Christ. With that membership comes the responsibility of helping Jesus in his saving work.

Your teacher will make the sign of the cross on your forehead with oil and say a blessing. It is the same blessing that the priest or deacon prayed when you were anointed with chrism at Baptism.

As Christ was anointed priest, prophet, and king, so may you live always as a member of his Body.

From the RITE OF BAPTISM

WITH YOUR FAMILY

You feel good about yourself when someone says, "Good job!" or "I'm proud of you." Your belief in yourself and your abilities is confirmed and strengthened. Think about how you can confirm and strengthen members of your family using words alone. When members of your family do something for you, be sure to say "thank you." Let them know how much you appreciate what they do for you.

PRIEST, PROPHET, KING

1. The work of the priest is to help people turn to God in prayer. Tell one way you can do this work.

2. The work of the prophet is to call people to follow God's Word and to be fair and just. Tell one way you can do this work.

3. The work of the king is to lead people to live together peacefully and to care for those in need. Tell one way you can do this work.

▼ REVIEW CHAPTER 9 ....

CATHOLICS BELIEVE

1. The sacrament of Confirmation seals and completes Baptism.
2. In Confirmation, the gifts of the Holy Spirit are given to strengthen the Christian to follow Jesus.
3. Confirmation is one of the three sacraments of initiation.

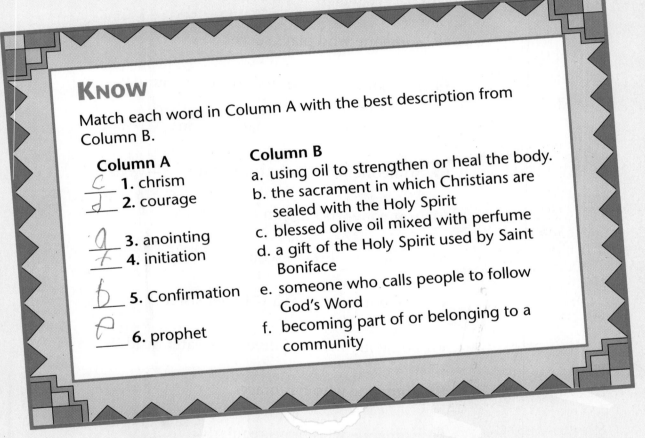

KNOW

Match each word in Column A with the best description from Column B.

Column A

___C___ 1. chrism

___d___ 2. courage

___a___ 3. anointing

___f___ 4. initiation

___b___ 5. Confirmation

___e___ 6. prophet

Column B

a. using oil to strengthen or heal the body.
b. the sacrament in which Christians are sealed with the Holy Spirit
c. blessed olive oil mixed with perfume
d. a gift of the Holy Spirit used by Saint Boniface
e. someone who calls people to follow God's Word
f. becoming part of or belonging to a community

SUNDAY MASS

One of the gifts of the Holy Spirit is wonder and awe in the presence of the Lord. Your parish church is one place where you come into the presence of the Lord. The art, music, flowers, banners, and other decorations you see there are meant to help you celebrate the mystery and wonder of God.

At Mass this Sunday, make a list of the many different things you see that suggest the greatness of God. Be prepared to describe at least one object and explain its use.

FROM MANY, ONE

Together, you are Christ's body.

1 CORINTHIANS 12:27

CONTENT KEYS

1. Jesus joins his life to yours in Communion
2. Eucharist unites you to Jesus and the Church.
3. Eucharist is one of the three sacraments of Initiation.

TWO PLUS TWO EQUALS ONE

Search among your classmates to find people who fit each of the following descriptions. When you find the right person, ask him or her to sign your textbook next to the description. Try to get a different name for each line.

❶. someone who plays soccer

❷. someone who goes to Mass every Sunday

❸. someone who takes piano lessons

❹. someone who likes green beans

❺. someone who has an older brother

❻. someone who is a scout

❼. someone who has a younger sister

❽. someone who can dive into water head first

❾. someone who has braces

❿. someone who prays regularly

The signatures you collected reveal a mystery. You and your classmates have many different interests, talents, and experiences. Yet with all your differences, you come together for the same purpose. Together you are one class.

1. **What are some of the things that unite the many people in your class into one group?**
2. **What are two signs that show that your class is united?**

ONE, THOUGH MANY

Each Sunday, Catholics gather together as one body to celebrate the Mass and eat the Body and Blood of Christ. This sacrament is known as the **Eucharist.**

The Eucharist is celebrated using bread and wine. Through God's grace, the bread and wine become our spiritual food. The bread and wine are signs that although the Church is made up of many people, it is one in the Body of Christ.

Bread begins in a wheat field. Each stalk of wheat produces several ears. Each ear is made up of many separate kernels. The threshing machine separates the kernels from the stalks.

At the mill, the separate kernels of wheat are ground between heavy rollers. The outer skins, called husks or chaff, are thrown away. What remains is ground finely into flour.

Flour is mixed with water to make the dough for unleavened bread, the kind used for Communion. Yeast and sugar can be added to make the bread rise.

After the dough is shaped into loaves and baked in the oven, it becomes fresh bread. What has happened to the wheat?

WINE

Wine begins in a vineyard. Each grapevine produces many bunches of grapes. Each bunch is made up of many separate grapes. Harvesters cut the bunches from the vines.

At the winery, the bunches of grapes are crushed. The stems, seeds, and sometimes the skins are discarded. Sometimes the juice that is left is blended with the juice of other kinds of grapes.

The grape juice is aged in barrels. Natural yeasts and sugars in the juice help it ferment. Wine used for the Eucharist must be made from pure grape juice, with nothing added.

After the fermented grape juice has aged, it is bottled as wine.

What has happened to the grapes?

SPECIAL WORDS

The word **eucharist** is used to describe both the Mass and the Body and Blood of Christ. The word *eucharist* comes from a Greek word meaning "offering thanks." The Eucharist is a sacrament of initiation.

SIGNS OF UNITY

CREATE AN IMAGE THAT SHOWS BREAD AND WINE AS A SIGN OF UNITY.

EUCHARIST: A SIGN OF UNITY

Ann washed her face and quickly brushed her hair. She was finishing just as her mom called her. "Come on, honey, time to get going."

Mrs. Keenan folded the morning paper and carried her coffee cup to the sink. Then she fished her keys out of her purse and headed for the door.

Jack Tomasi walked out to the driveway. "What a beautiful morning for golf," he thought. He slid into the driver's seat of the van where his wife, Jill, and their children were waiting. "What a beautiful morning to praise the Lord," he said.

Through the Eucharist the people of the church, though many, become one.

Saint Paul wrote to the Christian community at Corinth, "Because the loaf of bread is one, we, though many, are one body, for we all partake of the one loaf" *(1 Corinthians 10:17)*.

ONE LOAF

At church, Ann and her mom, and the Tomasis joined many other people in prayer and song. They listened to the Scriptures and offered one another a sign of peace. They shared the Body and Blood of Christ in the Eucharist.

By eating and drinking at the Table of the Lord, you become one not only with Jesus, but with all members of the Church. You are united with all the followers of Jesus—the ones standing next to you at Mass and all the Catholics around the world whom you will never meet in person.

Before receiving Holy Communion, Catholics must fast for one hour, be free from mortal sin, and seek to live in charity and love with their neighbors. People who are conscious of mortal sin must first celebrate God's forgiveness in the sacrament of Reconciliation before receiving Holy Communion.

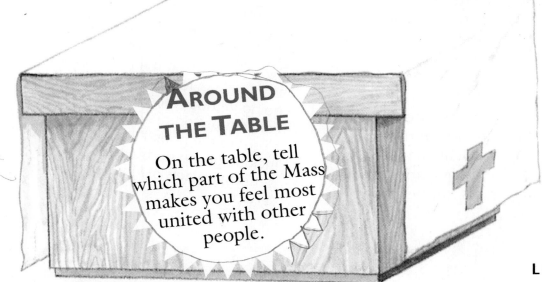

AROUND THE TABLE

On the table, tell which part of the Mass makes you feel most united with other people.

THE BODY OF CHRIST

In the sacrament of the Eucharist, you are united with Jesus. During the Mass, the bread and wine, the signs of many becoming one, become the Body and Blood of Christ. When you receive the Eucharist, the priest or eucharistic minister says to you: "the Body of Christ" or "the Blood of Christ." You say, "Amen!"

When you eat the Bread, and drink the Cup, Jesus joins his life to your life. You are in communion with him. You live in him, and he lives in you *(John 6:56)*. Jesus gives you the strength to follow him and to carry his love into the rest of your life.

It is because you are united with Jesus that you are also united with other Christians. It is in the sharing of the one loaf and the one cup that Christians come together as the Body of Christ in the world. The Eucharist is not just a *sign* of unity; it *creates* unity in Jesus.

SACRAMENTS OF BELONGING

Sixteen hundred years ago, Saint Augustine, a very wise teacher, compared breadmaking to belonging to the Church. Augustine opened his hand to show newly baptized Christians some grains of wheat. "You are like these grains of wheat," he said. "The grinding of the wheat is like the **fasting** and **penance** you did to prepare yourselves to follow Jesus. The water that binds the flour together is the water of Baptism. And the fire that bakes the dough is the fire of the Holy Spirit. The finished bread is the Eucharist."

Saint Augustine's comparison describes the three sacraments of initiation. Through Baptism, Confirmation, and Eucharist, you are made part of the Body of Christ.

SPECIAL WORDS

Fasting and **penance** are practices that train Christians to follow Jesus. Fasting is going without food in order to concentrate on prayer and to be closer to the poor. Penance can include giving up treats or performing acts of kindness or service.

RECIPE FOR UNITY

Follow the illustrated recipe for unity on this page. As you go along, tell how you can do each of these things.

Listen. When you listen, give the speaker a chance to say what he or she wants—don't interrupt. Listen for both the meaning and the feelings behind the words.

Share. Jesus encouraged his followers to share what they have with others. Share your time and smiles as well as your possessions.

Accept others. Be open to other people's ideas and solutions. Don't act like your way is the only way.

Pray. Talk to Jesus as a friend. Tell him your worries, your hopes, and your dreams. Ask him for his help—for yourself and for others.

Work together. The Church is a community gathered together in the name of Jesus. Pitch in and help when and where you are needed.

1. **What happens to the bread and wine at Mass?**
2. **Explain two ways in which the Eucharist is a sign of unity.**

One in Christ

Saint Augustine said that you are like a grain of wheat. Wheat has a hard shell that must be removed before it can be ground. What are some of the "hard shells" in your life that prevent you from following Jesus?

You can use the "Recipe for Unity" to help you follow Jesus. Learn to cooperate. Ask yourself two questions: What needs to be done? What can I do to help? Listen carefully to instructions and then follow them. Be open to new ideas and new ways of doing things. Do your best to get along with other people.

Hard Shells

What I Can Do to Remove the Hard Shells

IN COMMUNION

The same word that you use for being one with Jesus in the Eucharist—Communion—also describes your relationship with all other members of the Church.

Explain how you could be in communion in each of the situations described in the chart below. Use the ingredients for unity—listening, sharing, accepting others' ideas, praying, and working together—to provide solutions.

PROBLEM	SOLUTION
Your coach says, "Here's how to run this play."	
Your school needs volunteers to pick up trash.	
You are worried about your grandma, who is sick.	
You and your sister both want to sit in the front seat of the car.	

PRAYER AFTER COMMUNION

Use the following prayer to offer thanks to God.

Lord, may the Eucharist be our helmet of faith and our shield of good will. May it bring us love and patience, humility and obedience, and growth in the power to do good. May it unite us more closely to you, and lead us to everlasting light and joy with you. Amen.

SAINT THOMAS AQUINAS

WITH YOUR FAMILY

Your family has its own signs of unity. Which of these does your family do: eat dinner together, talk about what happened during the day, pray together, attend Mass together, work together to keep the household running smoothly? With your family, plan a time for family prayer. Listen to everyone's ideas. Then work together to make it happen.

▼REVIEW CHAPTER 10 ....

CATHOLICS BELIEVE

1. The Eucharist is a sacrament of initiation.
2. The bread and wine at the Eucharist become the Body and Blood of Christ.
3. Through the Eucharist, Christians become the Body of Christ.
4. When you receive the Eucharist, you are one with Jesus and with all members of the Church.

KNOW

1. Bread and wine are _____ of unity.
2. Baptism, Confirmation, and _____ are the sacraments of initiation.
3. In Saint Augustine's story, water stood for _____, fire stood for _____, and the finished bread was a sign of the _____.
4. _____ means being one with Jesus in the Eucharist, and being united with one another.
5. Saint Paul wrote that Christians are part of one _____.
6. In the Eucharist you eat the _____ and _____ of Christ.

SUNDAY MASS

When you go to Communion this Sunday, listen for when the priest or eucharistic minister says to you, "the Body of Christ." Look up and say "Amen!" in a clear, strong voice. In doing this, you show that you are part of Jesus' community. Hold up your hands to receive the Eucharist. Carefully place the host on your tongue. After Communion, thank Jesus for all the people who are united with you. Thank Jesus for living in you.

CONTENT KEYS

1. **Jesus offered people forgiveness from sin.**
2. **Reconciliation celebrates God's mercy.**
3. **Reconciliation is a sacrament of healing.**

Above all, let your love for one another be strong, because love wipes out sins.

From 1 PETER 4:8

THE CAMEL'S NOSE

Obbie the camel driver was asleep in his tent. Suddenly, Amer, his lead camel, stuck his nose under the flap of the tent. "Master," the camel said, "I am cold. Please let me put my head inside your tent."

Obbie shrugged, "Oh, all right. But just your head."

Obbie was dreaming of diamonds when Amer asked, "Master, my neck is cold. Please let me put it in the tent as well."

"Very well," replied Obbie, who rolled over and was soon snoring.

An hour later, Amer cleared his throat. "Kind master, I am very uncomfortable standing this way. Allow me to bring my front legs into the tent."

"You may do so," Obbie answered, moving over a little to make room for the camel.

Obbie was just dozing off when the camel spoke up again, "Generous master, the cold air is rushing into the tent. Permit me to come all the way in and close the flap."

"Very well," Obbie responded.

The camel pushed his way into the tent. Now the tent was too crowded for both Obbie and his beast.

"There is not enough room for both of us in this small tent," pointed out the camel. "Since you are smaller than I, you should stand outside." And Amer pushed Obbie out the door.

Standing outside shivering in the cold, Obbie said to himself, "I can see now that it is better to stop bad things before they get started."

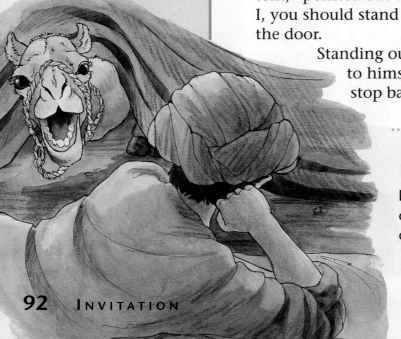

Nosin' In

Describe how a little thing can get out of control. What big problems can a little thing cause?

STARTING OVER

The tale of Obbie and his camel is a fable. But the following story is true. It is about a man who let his bad habits get out of control.

Charles de Foucauld grew up in a rich and noble French family. Charles was spoiled as a child and thought only of himself. When he didn't get his own way, he quickly became angry. Charles let his little bad habits grow and grow until he became a selfish and greedy young man. He wasted his time and money on wild parties and drinking. He turned away from God. His behavior hurt others and was hurting him, too.

Feeling bored, Charles traveled around the world looking for something to make him happy. In the North African desert country of Morocco, Charles had a conversion, or change of heart. The simple life of the people, so different from his own, appealed to him. Where his many possessions left him feeling empty, their simple life filled his heart.

Charles returned to France, but he did not forget the desert. He wanted to find that peace for himself. He now knew that his old friends and his old way of life would never satisfy him. Charles told this to a friend, Marie de Bondy, who convinced him to take the next step and return to God and to the Catholic faith.

In 1886, Charles returned to the Church. He knelt and humbly confessed his sins to the priest. The priest gave him absolution and offered forgiveness in God's name. Charles had found God's forgiveness and peace. From then on, Charles's life was guided by the love of God.

A New Life

In time, Charles became a priest and returned to the Sahara. He wanted to share all the goodness he had found in Jesus with the Touareg people. He dreamed of starting a community of brothers who would live as simply as the people they served.

Charles learned the languages of the Touareg people and he respected their customs. He dressed in a simple robe of rough white cloth and wore sandals that were cracked with age.

The Touaregs, who were Muslims, respected Charles as a holy man. They knew he shared every scrap of his food with the poor, and that he spent long days and nights in prayer. The Touaregs listened politely when Charles talked to them about Jesus Christ. But they kept their own ways.

By the time Charles died in 1916, he had not made a single convert among the Touaregs. Instead, it was Charles who had changed. He had become a saint.

Today, five communities of religious men and women work and pray as Charles did in the desert.

1. **What happened to Charles de Foucauld when he let bad habits and sins take control of his life?**
2. **What caused Charles to make a change in his life?**
3. **How did Charles's life change after he accepted God's love and forgiveness?**

In His Shoes

Charles de Foucauld inspired many people by his behavior. Explain why you think people were inspired by Charles.

SIN AND FORGIVENESS

As you have seen, little things can turn into major problems. Sometimes when little things get out of control, they can lead you away from God. Anything that leads you from God is a sin. The word *sin* means "missing the mark."

The little things that lead you from God are known as venial sins. These are actions, thoughts, or words that weaken your relationship with God and with the community. Venial sins cannot destroy your relationship with God, no matter how many you commit. However, these little sins can lead you to much more serious sins, which can come between you and God.

Sins that destroy your relationship with God are called mortal or deadly, because they kill the life of God within you. Mortal sins don't happen by accident. For a sin to be mortal, it must meet these three conditions:

1. *The action must be seriously wrong.*
2. *You must know it is seriously wrong.*
3. *You must freely choose to do it anyway.*

Charles de Foucauld committed a mortal sin when he decided he didn't need God anymore and left the Catholic Church. He willingly chose to turn his back on God.

While it is important to recognize what you do that leads you from God, Jesus said you also need to recognize why you do wrong. It is a bad attitude that leads you to be selfish, angry, greedy, dishonest, jealous, spiteful, or mean. (See *Matthew 15:19*.) By contrast, a good attitude can lead you to be loving, joyful, peaceful, patient, generous, truthful, kind, forgiving, chaste, and caring.

Jesus Offers Forgiveness

Simon was an important man in town. He had invited Jesus and a few close friends to dinner. Simon and his guests were just about to begin a fine meal when they heard a commotion outside. Then a woman burst into the dining room and threw herself before Jesus, sobbing quietly. As her tears fell upon his feet, she wiped them with her long hair and then poured sweet-smelling oil on them. Jesus did not pull back from the woman.

The other guests were stunned. This woman had a very bad reputation, and everyone there knew it. A real prophet would condemn her for what she had done, Simon thought.

Jesus turned and looked at the frown on Simon's face. "This woman is showing sorrow for her sins," said Jesus. "She has felt God's forgiveness, and so her heart is full of love." Then Jesus said to the woman, "Your sins are forgiven. Go in peace."

Based on LUKE 7:36–39, 47–48

Reconciliation

Jesus knew how small things could lead to much bigger problems. He listened to people's problems and then told them to live their lives differently. Jesus offered people reconciliation. He helped them regain control over their lives.

Jesus continues to offer you forgiveness and healing today. In his name, the Church forgives you from your sins in the sacrament of Reconciliation. This is a sacrament of healing. In the sacrament, you admit what you have done wrong, say that you are sorry for your actions, and promise to try and change your behavior—to get the little things in your life back under control. The sacrament of Reconciliation is also called the sacrament of Penance.

Venial sins are forgiven by receiving the Eucharist or the sacrament of Reconciliation. Because they are much more serious, you are obliged to confess all mortal sins. Regular confession of all sins in the sacrament of Reconciliation is a spiritually beneficial practice.

CELEBRATING THE SACRAMENT

You celebrate God's loving forgiveness in the sacrament of Reconciliation. In this sacrament, you confess what you have done wrong and show contrition, or sorrow, for your sins. You promise to turn away from sin and to follow Jesus better. The priest gives you a penance to help you make satisfaction for or undo the wrong you have done.

"Through the ministry of the Church may God give you pardon and peace, and I absolve you from your sins in the name of the Father, and of the Son, and of the Holy Spirit."

A Case to Consider

Ronda is proud of being the fastest runner in her class. In the last race, Hannah, the new girl, beat Ronda by one pace. To get even, Ronda started a rumor about Hannah, telling everyone that Hannah was a whole year older and was repeating fifth grade.

- Why do you think Ronda told lies about Hannah? What was her attitude? Was it a sin?
- What do you think Ronda's lies do to her relationship with God?
- What can Ronda do to correct the problem she caused and gain forgiveness?

FOLLOWING Jesus

Jesus offers forgiveness to everyone. Followers of Jesus are asked to forgive others as Jesus did. When you've been hurt, it's not easy to offer forgiveness and really mean it. Start with little things. Try not to hold a grudge. Offer a handshake instead of a fist. Smile even when you feel like frowning. By these little gestures you say "I forgive you." In this way you give someone else a fresh start.

1. **What makes thoughts and actions sins?**
2. **How does Jesus forgive sins today?**
3. **Give two good reasons for celebrating the sacrament of Reconciliation often.**

You Forgive

Jesus said that his followers must forgive as they are forgiven. Forgiving others is easier to do if you remember that you're not perfect and that you've been forgiven by a lot by other people and especially by God. Explain how you could show forgiveness in each of the following situations.

1. A sixth grader laughed when you tripped in the lunchroom. _____
_____

2. A friend broke your best pen. _____
_____

3. The neighbor threw rocks at your puppy. _____
_____

4. Your little sister tattled on you. _____
_____

5. A teammate called you a name when you struck out. _____
_____

Read the story of forgiveness Jesus told in Matthew 18: 23–35. In your own words, write a sentence telling what you've learned from Jesus' story. _____
_____

With All My Heart

In the heart, write your own prayer asking Jesus for forgiveness for your sins. Ask for his help in turning your heart to him and making a fresh start. When you have finished writing, pray your prayer aloud, then exchange a sign of peace with your classmates.

WITH YOUR FAMILY

When something goes wrong at home, what makes things go from bad to worse? Here are a few things you can practice to keep the camel's nose out of your family's tent.
• Admit your own faults.
• Take a moment to cool down.
• Think before you speak.
• Don't hold a grudge.
• Pray.

CATHOLICS BELIEVE

1. The sacrament of Reconciliation is a celebration of God's loving forgiveness.
2. In Reconciliation, the wounds of sin and division are healed.
3. Through Reconciliation you are reunited with God and with the Church.

KNOW

Choose **T** if the statement is true. Choose **F** if the statement is false.

T F 1. The sacrament of Reconciliation forgives your sins.

T F 2. Jesus forgave the sinful woman because she showed sorrow for her sins.

T F 3. You can commit a mortal sin accidentally.

T F 4. In the sacrament of Reconciliation, the Church celebrates Jesus' healing and forgiveness.

T F 5. Charles de Foucauld was a sinner who changed his life.

T F 6. Venial sins are forgiven through receiving the Eucharist.

SUNDAY MASS

After the opening greeting of the Mass, the priest and the people ask God for mercy and forgiveness. This is the Penitential Rite. One form of the Penitential Rite is the prayer of contrition called the Confiteor. It begins, "I confess to almighty God, and to you, my brothers and sisters." Another form of the Penitential Rite is the litany, "Lord, have mercy." This Sunday, ask God to forgive you of your personal sins during the Penitential Rite.

12

CONTENT KEYS

1. **Jesus healed the sick.**
2. **Anointing of the Sick celebrates God's healing power.**
3. **Anointing of the Sick is celebrated with prayer, touch, and oil.**

LOVE AND MERCY

Pray for one another, that you may be healed. The fervent prayer of a good person is very powerful.

From JAMES 5:16

BE A HEALER

Everyone is sick or sad at some time in life. People often send cards to cheer up a sick or sad person. Each of the people below needs cheering. Choose an appropriate card and write the person's name on the envelope. On the card describe the kind of healing you think the person needs.

1. Morgan went to camp with her best friend. She got homesick and really missed her family.
2. Catherine and her sister Theresa had a terrible fight. Catherine got so mad that she refused to speak to Theresa for a whole week.
3. Ryan's grandma lives alone. Most days she doesn't feel well enough to go out.
4. Marcus was riding his bike when he was hit by a car. Now he has a broken leg.

I Really Miss You

Get Well Soon

Thinking of You

I'M SORRY !

Get-Well Card

What message of concern could you share with a person who is sick or alone? Write your message on the card.

Get Well

IN THE NAME OF JESUS

Ezra could not walk. Everyday his brothers carried him to a spot outside of the Temple's Beautiful Gate to beg for money from worshipers.

Amid the din of people, two men noticed Ezra calling out, "Spare some coins for a crippled beggar and thank the Almighty for allowing you to walk."

Unlike other people who hurriedly tossed a coin into the old man's lap, Peter and John stopped and looked straight at Ezra. As he turned away from their gaze, he continued his chant "Alms for the poor."

"Look at us," said Peter, looking at Ezra and seeing a face filled with much pain and loneliness. "I have neither silver nor gold, but what I do have, I give you," he said, reaching out his hand. "In the name of Jesus Christ the Nazarean, stand up and walk."

Everything happened so fast. Ezra heard the words and reached out to grab Peter's hand, but his mind was not on the two men. All his attention was focused on the incredible warmth rushing through his legs. It was unlike anything he had ever felt before.

Whoa! Ezra thought. I'm standing! I'm walking! When he realized he was healed, he began jumping and shouting for joy at the top of his lungs, "Thanks be to Jesus. Thank you, God. Just look at me now, people!"

In fact, everyone was already looking at Ezra in total amazement as he went off with Peter and John, dancing and praising God. By the time they reached the next gate, the crowd had become too large to ignore. Peter turned and spoke to them.

"God has done this to glorify his son, Jesus. By faith in the name of Jesus, this man whom you all know has been made strong and restored to perfect health. All that Jesus asks is that you repent and believe in him."

Based on ACTS 3:1–10, 16

A Sign of God's Love

Peter and John got into a great deal of trouble for speaking this way. The Temple guards immediately arrested and jailed them for teaching about Jesus. But the people were praising God so loudly for healing the beggar, the guards released Peter and John the next day.

Peter and John were doing what Jesus told them to do in Matthew 25:31–46. As a sign of God's love, they cared for the sick and relieved people's suffering in Jesus' name. Sometimes their actions led to physical healing, as in the case of the beggar at the Beautiful Gate. More often their actions led to spiritual healing and a deep awareness of God's love.

Long after Peter, John, and the other Apostles had died, Jesus' healing continued in the Church through the sacrament of the Anointing of the Sick. All followers of Jesus—yes, even you!—are called to heal in the name of Jesus.

1. Explain how Peter and John's healing of the crippled man was a sign of God's love.
2. What does it feel like to be cured of an illness or relieved of a serious problem?
3. Give an example of how people who promote healing are signs of God's love.

THE PRAYER OF FAITH

READ JAMES 5:13–15. IN YOUR OWN WORDS, DESCRIBE THE ORIGIN OF THE SACRAMENT OF THE ANOINTING OF THE SICK.

THE MINISTRY OF HEALING

At 5 o'clock, Edel Quinn covered her typewriter and quickly cleared off her desk. The young secretary wrapped up a bright bouquet of flowers and put on her coat and hat. As she walked briskly to the bus stop, she thought of the Virgin Mary, who traveled in haste to help her cousin Elizabeth. Like Mary, Edel was eager to help.

Edel knocked lightly and then popped her head into old Mrs. Burke's small dreary boarding house room. Soon the young woman and the lonely old woman were laughing together.

When she was 19, Edel had joined the Legion of Mary. The purpose of the group was to bring spiritual help however and wherever it was needed. Every evening Edel visited the sick and the elderly. Sometimes she helped teenage mothers learn to care for their children.

Beneath her cheerfulness, Edel had a secret.

She herself was very sick. The disease made her weak, and there was no cure. But Edel wasn't thinking about herself. Like Mary, she hurried to help others.

When she was 29, Edel Quinn quit her job and left her home in Ireland. As a member of the Legion of Mary, she went to Africa to spread the Church's work of caring. Edel was overjoyed at this opportunity.

Even though she was getting weaker, Edel traveled all over East Africa, venturing to places no European woman had ever been. She always kept her sense of humor, bouncing over the rough roads in an old Ford she called her Rolls Royce.

Edel died of tuberculosis in Nairobi, Kenya, in 1944, at the age of 36. Thousands of people joined the funeral procession for a woman who had touched them all with the healing of Jesus.

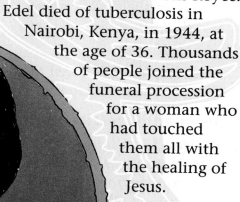

ANOINTING OF THE SICK

The Church celebrates the sacrament of the Anointing of the Sick for people who need healing. The sacrament is celebrated with anyone who is seriously ill, who faces surgery, or who is frail because of old age. In the sacrament, the Church prays for the sick, anoints the person with oil, and asks Jesus to heal him or her. The sacrament is often celebrated in church, but it is also celebrated in hospitals, nursing homes, and even in one's own home.

BARBARA'S ANOINTING

Barbara: *Why do I have to have this stupid operation tomorrow?*

Dad: *This operation will make you breathe much easier and allow you to do more things with your friends.*

Barbara: *But how come I'm getting anointed?*

Dad: *Anointing is a sign that God's strength is with you to make you well.*

Mom and brother: *We're here, too.*

Father Tim: *It looks like everyone is ready. Let's begin our celebration with a short reading from the Gospel of Luke. "After sunset all who had friends who were sick with various diseases brought them to Jesus; he placed his hand on every one of them and healed them all" (Luke 4:40).*

Father Tim: *Through this holy anointing may the Lord in his love and mercy help you with the grace of the Holy Spirit.*

Everyone: *Amen.*

Father Tim: *May the Lord who frees you from sin save you and raise you up.*

Everyone: *Amen.*

Barbara: *Just three months since my surgery and I feel great! Thank you, God!*

FOLLOWING Jesus

As a follower of Jesus, you, too, are sent to heal. You can do that by trying to understand what other people feel. You can do a lot of healing simply by being a good listener and doing little things to help other people feel better: fluff a pillow, give a drink of water, or read a newspaper article aloud. You will be surprised at how good you will feel after you bring God's healing touch to others.

1. **What did Barbara's family and friends do to help her? What did the Church do to help her?**
2. **What did Edel Quinn do to bring the healing touch of Jesus to others?**

Healers

Make a short list of people you know who help people who are hurt, sick, lonely, or sad. Explain how they help others.

Healing Person	His or Her Healing Work

YOU ARE A HEALER

You don't have to be a nurse or a doctor to care for a person who is sick. You don't have to be a priest to bring God's healing to others. All you have to do is show that you care.

Think of people in your own family, school, parish, or neighborhood who are sick, lonely, grieving, or left out. Is there an elderly person who would enjoy a visit and a game of checkers? Does your little brother or sister need you to be a pal? What can you do to reach out to them?

Person	Need	How I Can Reach Out

Visiting the sick and praying for them are works of mercy (see page 235 of *I Am a Catholic*). If a member of your family is sick or elderly, or lives in a nursing home, plan a family visit soon. If the person lives too far away to visit, telephone or send a card. At meal or night prayers, pray with your family for people who are sick, especially for those you know and love.

PRAY FOR THE SICK

Stand with your class in a circle. Think of a person you know who needs healing. Close your eyes and picture that person. Go around the circle. When it's your turn, say a short prayer for this person aloud. (You do not have to name the person, but you may.) After each prayer say, "Lord, grant your healing and peace."

▼ REVIEW CHAPTER 12

CATHOLICS BELIEVE

1. In the sacrament of the Anointing of the Sick, the Church continues the healing work of Jesus Christ.
2. In the sacrament of Anointing, people are anointed with oil on their head and hands. The priest lays hands upon them and prays for their recovery.

KNOW

Complete each sentence by underlining the right word in the parentheses.

1. The sacrament of the Anointing of the Sick can bring both physical and spiritual (healing, meaning) to the sick.
2. Saint James told Church members to pray over and anoint (the sick, the poor).
3. Edel Quinn joined the (convent, Legion of Mary) to help others spiritually.
4. During the Anointing of the Sick, the priest traces the sign of the cross on the person's head and hands with (oil, water).

SUNDAY MASS

At Mass this Sunday, pay close attention to the General Intercessions, or Prayers of the Faithful, which are said after the Creed. These prayers are for the needs of the Church and often include a prayer for the sick of the parish. Listen to each prayer and answer "Lord, hear our prayer." In doing this, you join with the prayer of the Church for those who are sick and suffering.

What's My Sign?

In religious art, saints have often been shown with objects or symbols that tell something about their lives. The object of this game is to match the saints with their signs.

Saint Agnes was 12 or 13 years old when she died as one of the martyrs of the early Church. Because she was known for her purity and goodness, a stone covering her grave was inscribed with the words "most holy lamb."

Saint Augustine was a generous, friendly, down-to-earth kind of guy. When he taught about God, he was a brilliant speaker and writer who soared like an eagle.

Saint Camillus founded a religious order of men who were the first battlefield medics. Wearing white robes marked with a red cross, they also nursed plague victims and sick people in hospitals.

Saint Martin, an officer in the Roman army, came upon a beggar who was shivering in the cold. Martin cut his heavy cloak in two and gave half to the beggar. That night, in a dream, Martin saw Jesus wearing the cloak.

While the music was playing at her wedding reception, **Saint Cecilia** sang a song asking God to keep her heart pure. Later, composers wrote beautiful music for her feast day, and Cecilia became the patron saint of all musicians.

Saint Elizabeth of Hungary was a queen who carried food to the poor and hungry people of her land. She never stopped trusting in the goodness of God.

Saint Francis of Assisi once preached to a flock of birds. He told them to praise God for the trees, rivers, and air. All the birds listened until he gave them his blessing.

Saint Joseph was a good father who taught the boy Jesus how to use all the tools of his trade.

Saint Maria Goretti was 12 years old when she was murdered by a 19-year-old man. Eight years later, the man saw Maria in a dream, offering him white lilies. He changed his life and asked forgiveness from his sin.

Saint Peter recognized Jesus as the Messiah, the son of God who was to come into the world. In return Jesus said that he would give Peter the keys to the kingdom of heaven.

Saint Stephen was filled with the Holy Spirit and spoke courageously about Jesus. The Jewish leaders dragged him out of the city and stoned him. As he was dying, Stephen called out, "Lord Jesus, forgive them."

Saint Teresa of Avila was a beautiful and lively girl who became a leader of the Carmelite religious order. Teresa wrote her autobiography and several books about prayer that have inspired and taught many people.

Saint Thérèse of Lisieux became a very great saint by doing little things, even boring chores, with a lot of love. Thérèse promised to continue to do good things after her death and said she would send them down like a shower of roses upon the earth.

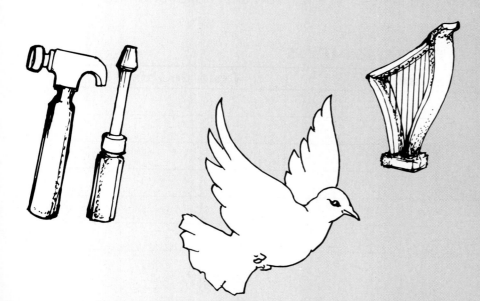

LEARNING

1. What are sacraments?
Sacraments are signs and celebrations of God's power and love. Through the sacraments, Catholics share in God's life.

2. What are the sacraments of initiation?
The sacraments of initiation are Baptism, Confirmation, and Eucharist.

3. What is the Eucharist?
The Eucharist is the Body and Blood of Christ.

4. What are the sacraments of healing?
Reconciliation and Anointing of the Sick are the sacraments of healing.

5. What happens in the sacrament of Reconciliation?
The sacrament of Reconciliation is a celebration of God's loving forgiveness. Through Reconciliation, sin is forgiven and a Christian is reunited with God and with the Church.

6. Why does the Church celebrate the sacrament of the Anointing of the Sick?
In the sacrament of the Anointing of the Sick, the Church continues the healing work of Jesus Christ by caring for those who are sick or weak.

PRAYING

All: Have mercy on us, O God, in your goodness.

1: Wash away our sins, Lord, and let us hear the sounds of joy and gladness.

2: Create in us clean hearts, O God, and renew our spirits within us.

All: Have mercy on us, O God, in your goodness.

3: Never make us leave your presence, and do not take your Holy Spirit from us.

4: We will teach everyone about your love, and sinners will return to you.

All: Have mercy on us, O God, in your goodness.

Based on PSALM 51

LIVING

The sacraments are signs that God's grace is active in the world. On the chart, identify the sacrament or sacraments you think is seen in the action. Then note how you can carry out this action.

ASKING

1. What do I do that shows that I belong to the Church?
2. How am I a sign of Christ?

LIVING THE SACRAMENTS

Sacramental Action	Sacrament	I can do this!
Be a healer for someone		
Forgive someone		
Ask for personal forgiveness		
Make a good decision		
Be friendly and welcoming		
Share God's gifts with others		

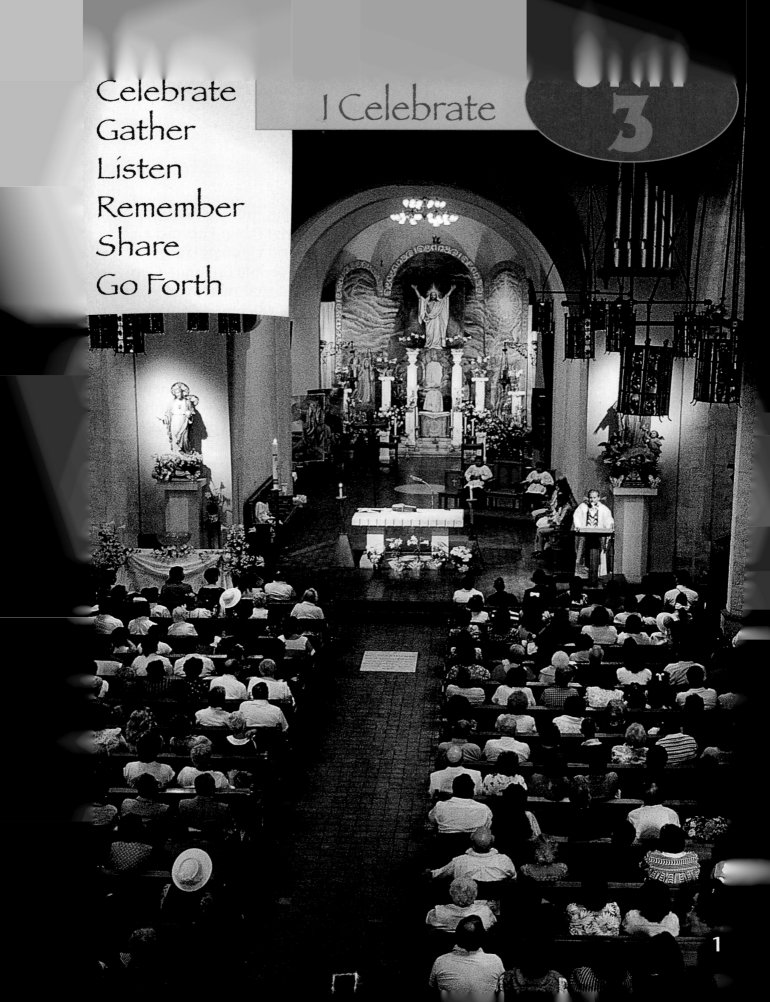

Celebrate
Gather
Listen
Remember
Share
Go Forth

CELEBRATE

CONTENT KEYS

1. **Creation is a celebration of God's love.**
2. **The Church is a celebrating community.**
3. **You celebrate holy times in a holy place, a church.**

I rejoiced because they said to me, "We will go up to the house of the Lord."

PSALM 122:1

LET'S CELEBRATE

A fierce dragon leaps down the street, weaving from side to side in the parade. Bang! Bang! Bang! Firecrackers explode. Boom! Bong! Gongs and cymbals crash.

Each year, millions of people celebrate Chinese New Year. There is a ritual that many Chinese people follow before they celebrate. On the last day of the year, they pay all their debts. Then they seal their doors, and the family settles down to an all-night feast. In the morning, the seals are broken and the doors are opened to the brand new year! The celebrations include parades with lion dancers, children carrying lanterns, and, of course, the dragon, a symbol of strength and goodness.

Occurring between mid-January and mid-February, this festival is the celebration of the birth of a new year. To top it off, each person also celebrates his or her own birthday on that day. What a party!

You may or may not celebrate Chinese New Year, but you do celebrate a lot of other occasions. You celebrate special days with special people, often in special places.

I CELEBRATE

What does your family celebrate? What special things do you do on each of these days?

CELEBRATION	WE GATHER	WE REMEMBER	WE SHARE

HOLY TIMES

"That was nothing," boasted Samuel, skipping and spinning, showing his friend Jesus how the dance was done. "You have to be a kid to really know how to dance like David before the Lord."

Suddenly, Samuel halted his dancing. Raising both hands toward the direction of Jerusalem, he sang out loudly, "We shall go up with joy to the house of the Lord."

"On the third day of the journey, when we're about two hours away from the Temple," Samuel informed Jesus, "we all sing that song together. Then we will be at the very gates of the Temple."

Joseph put his strong hand on Jesus' shoulder, "Son when we get into Jerusalem, I want you to help me find the perfect lamb for the sacrifice. For this feast, we must make certain to do everything exactly as the Lord has commanded us through the great prophet Moses."

"You can just feel this is a wonderful and holy time, can't you?" said Samuel, looking at Jesus. "But what makes Passover the holiest of all the feasts?"

"That's easy," Jesus replied. "Don't you remember the story of the Exodus from Egypt? Passover is the holiest day because it's the time when we remember all the great things the Lord did to free our people from slavery in Egypt.

"On their journey, the Lord fed them with manna and gave them water when there was nothing to drink. The Lord guided our people through the desert with a pillar of cloud by day and a pillar of fire by night until they safely reached the Promised Land. But in all the remembering and celebrating we do," Jesus added, "we must never forget that Passover is a holy time because the Lord is right here, present with us."

"Wow," said Samuel, "I don't think the teachers at the Temple could have explained it better."

"Thank you, Samuel," said Jesus. "Perhaps we will listen to some of the teachers when we get to the Temple."

Inspired by
LUKE 2:41–42

THE LITURGICAL YEAR

Many years later, after the death and resurrection of Jesus, his followers began to celebrate their own feasts, or holy days. These feasts were different from the ones that Jesus had celebrated with his family and friends. The new feasts celebrated the great events and deeds of Jesus' life. Easter, the day of Jesus' resurrection, became the first and most important Christian holy day. Every Sunday (the day the Lord had risen) was celebrated as "little Easter."

In time, Christians realized that it was not possible to celebrate the important events of Christ's life in a few feast days. They needed a whole year to remember and celebrate what Jesus did. This yearly cycle of Christian feasts and seasons is called the liturgical year.

Christians celebrate many special feasts each year. Jesus' birth is remembered at Christmas. Mary's acceptance of God's will is celebrated on March 25, the feast of the Annunciation. In fact, on nearly every day of the year, the Church celebrates the life of someone who had a special relationship with God.

The liturgical year is divided into the six times of Advent, Christmas, Lent, The Triduum, Eastertime, and Ordinary Time.

1. **What feast do Christians celebrate on Sunday?**
2. **What are some of the feasts that Christians celebrate each year?**
3. **In what ways is the liturgical year like a regular calendar? In what ways is it different from a regular calendar?**

THIS PLACE IS HOLY

There are no limits to the number of holy places in the world. Any place you feel God's presence is holy. Any place God's saving love is revealed or any place you show your love for God and others is also holy.

Some places, however, are considered especially holy. For Christians, Moslems, and Jews, the city of Jerusalem is a very holy place. In Jerusalem, an amazing act of faith took place.

A HOLY PLACE

At God's command, Abraham took his son Isaac to the land of Moriah, to a high place that God pointed out to him, to sacrifice his son to the Lord. Isaac carried the wood for the sacrifice on his back. Abraham took the fire and the knife, and they started up the mountain. As the two walked together, Isaac asked, "Father, here are the fire and the wood, but where is the sheep for the sacrifice?"

"Son," Abraham replied, "God will provide the sheep." Abraham built an altar on the mountain and arranged the wood on it. Then he tied up his son Isaac and put him on top of the wood on the altar.

As Abraham reached for the knife, God intervened, "Do not lay your hand on the boy. Do not do the least thing to him. I know now that you love me, for you do not hold back your own beloved son."

Then Abraham spied a ram caught by his horns in a thick bush. He took the ram and offered it as a sacrifice. God promised to bless Abraham and to give him descendants as numerous as the stars of the sky and the sands of the seashore. It was on this holy place that the Temple of Solomon would be built.

From GENESIS 22:1–18

My Holy Place

Where have you felt God's presence?
Describe or draw a place that is holy to you.

My Father's House

The Temple in Jerusalem was the most holy place for the Jews of Jesus' time. The beautiful temple built by King Solomon had been destroyed by the Babylonians in 587 B.C. King Herod the Great built another temple on the same site. People traveled from all over the country to gather in Jerusalem. As a twelve-year-old boy, Jesus was eligible for the first time to enter the inner courts of the Temple with the men.

The Temple was a very large and beautiful building. Its white stone walls and gold decorations could be seen from far away, sitting on the hilltop and glistening in the sun. The Temple housed the Ark of the Covenant and contained the stone tablets with the Ten Commandments. Prayers and animal sacrifices were offered in the Temple.

A Place to Celebrate

The first followers of Jesus, who were Jews, continued to go to the Temple to pray. But they also gathered to celebrate the Lord's Supper, as Jesus had told them to do. At first they met in their homes and celebrated the Eucharist at the dinner table. Eventually, homes became too small for the growing community. They then began to meet in larger public buildings.

When being a Christian was made a crime punishable by death, Christians were forced to gather in secret places. Later, when Christianity became the official religion of Rome, Christians built large churches as their places of worship and celebration.

In Syria, at a place called Dura-Europos, the ruins of one of the house churches dating back to the time of the very early Christians were discovered. The ruins show a central courtyard with a fountain. Around the courtyard are many different rooms—for celebrating the Eucharist, for holding meetings, for instructing catechumens, and for celebrating Baptism.

FOLLOWING Jesus

Jesus often went away to quiet places to be alone with his Father. He also prayed at night or early in the morning, before the disciples were awake.

GOD IS HERE

God is everywhere, but people need a gathering place to celebrate and pray. Just as the Israelites worshiped in the Tent of Meeting in the desert, and later at the Temple in Jerusalem, Christians worship in a church. The word *church* comes from the Greek word meaning "belonging to God." The word *church* is used to describe both the building in which Christians worship and the Christian community itself. A church building is a holy place because of what the Christian people remember and celebrate there.

A TIME AND PLACE FOR GOD

Many passages in the Bible describe the importance of setting aside time and space for God. When you set aside a special time and space for God, you can examine the ordinary events and places in your life to see how God is present there.

Read the following passages from Scripture. What does each tell you about holy times and holy places?

Exodus 3:1–9

1 Kings 19:11–13

Psalm 27:4–6

Luke 11:1–13

Hebrews 4:9–11

You can take three steps to follow Jesus in prayer.

1. *Understand that spending time with God is important.*
2. *Make a definite plan. Set aside a time and place.*
3. *Do it. No excuses, no delays.*

Start by praying only a few minutes at a time. After a while, you will find yourself wanting to spend more time with God.

1. **What are two reasons why the site of the Temple is considered holy?**
2. **What makes a church a holy place?**

Your Dwelling Place

The psalms are songs of praise offered to God. A psalm is prayed each day at Mass. You can make praying the psalms a part of your daily prayer ritual.

Psalm 84 is one of the psalms Jesus would have sung on the way to Jerusalem. Pray this psalm with your classmates.

Group 1: *How lovely is your dwelling place, O Lord of Hosts! My soul yearns and pines for the courts of the Lord. My heart and my flesh cry out for the living God.*

Group 2: *Even the sparrow finds a home, and the swallow a nest in which she puts her young—your altars, O Lord of hosts, my King and my God!*

Group 1: *Happy are they who dwell in your house! Continually they praise you.*

Group 2: *I had rather one day in your courts than a thousand elsewhere; I had rather lie at the threshold of the house of my God than dwell in the tents of the wicked.*

Group 1: *For a sun and a shield is the Lord God; grace and glory he bestows.*

Group 2: *The Lord withholds no good thing from those who walk in sincerity.*

WITH YOUR FAMILY

Ask a parent or grandparent about your special family holiday customs. Try to find out how they got started, why your family does them, and what each means.

CATHOLICS BELIEVE

1. The Church is a celebrating community.
2. You celebrate holy times—feasts and seasons—in a holy place, a church.

KNOW

Carefully read each of the statements below. Choose **T** if the statement is true. Choose **F** if the statement is false.

 T **F** 1. Jesus celebrated Jewish festivals with his family and friends.

 T **F** 2. Christians gathered to celebrate the Eucharist at the Temple in Jerusalem.

 T **F** 3. God is present only in a church building.

 T **F** 4. Christian feasts commemorate events in the life of Jesus, Mary, and the saints.

 T **F** 5. Passover recalls the journey of God's People from slavery to freedom.

 T **F** 6. Christians remember Jesus' resurrection only once a year.

SUNDAY MASS

What Sunday in the liturgical year will the Church celebrate this week? Read the readings for this Sunday before going to Mass. What event or teaching in the life of Jesus is remembered and celebrated this week?

CONTENT KEYS

1. **The Catholic family gathers at Mass.**
2. **Introductory Rites begin the Mass.**
3. **Liturgy is the work of God's people.**

Shout joyfully to God, all you on earth, sing praise to the glory of God's name. Let all on earth worship and sing praise to God.

PSALM 66:1,2,4

FAMILY REUNION

"**W**hat do want for your birthday, Mama?" asked Lucia.

This year Mrs. Morales did not hesitate. "I've been thinking about that," she said eagerly. "I'm going to be eighty years old. It's time for something special.

"All I want," she continued, "is a family party. I want all my children and grandchildren to eat cake and ice cream with me."

Making Mrs. Morales' wish come true would not be easy. Her son Juan and his family lived in Mexico. Her other sons, Julio and Carlos, had quarreled with each other ten years ago. The reason for their argument was long forgotten, but the two brothers had not spoken to each other since.

Lucia helped her mother send invitations to all of the members of the Morales family. They would have a barbecue and birthday party in Lucia's backyard.

Slowly Lucia's brothers responded to the invitations. Everyone was coming, even Juan and his family. Julio and Carlos agreed to forget their feud for a day to celebrate with their mother.

On the day of the party, the family gathered at Lucia's for the festivities. Each person greeted Lucia with a big hug and a laugh, and greeted Mrs. Morales with a kiss on both cheeks. This is how they always began a celebration in the Morales family.

1. **What reasons did the Morales family have for gathering?**
2. **What did Lucia do to make everyone feel welcome?**

FAMILY GATHERING

The story of the Morales family can help you understand something about the Mass, the Catholic family gathering. Just as members of the Morales family gathered to celebrate Mrs. Morales' birthday, Catholics come together as one family to celebrate the Eucharist. And just as the Morales family used certain gestures of greeting when they gathered, Catholics use certain words and gestures to begin the Mass.

The Mass always begins with an entrance procession. The priest **celebrant** and the other ministers walk in together from the rear of the Church or from the **sacristy.** You stand and join in singing as they proceed to the altar. When the priest reaches the **sanctuary,** he kisses the altar. He then begins the Mass with the sign of the cross, saying, "In the name of the Father, and of the Son, and of the Holy Spirit." You make the sign of the cross with the priest and respond, "Amen." The priest then greets the community with a prayer asking for God's grace. The community returns the greeting "And also with you."

SPECIAL WORDS

The bishop, priest, or deacon who leads the community in prayer is called the **celebrant.** The **sacristy** is the small room where the priest prepares for Mass. The **sanctuary** is the area around the altar.

FOLLOWING Jesus

When you offer someone hospitality, you make him or her feel welcome. The word *hospitality* means "to give shelter." You will often see parishioners greeting people as they arrive for Mass. These people are ministers of hospitality. You can practice hospitality at Mass by greeting your friends, your acquaintances, and newcomers. You can practice hospitality at home, at school, and in your neighborhood by offering others the shelter of a smile or a kind word.

LORD, HAVE MERCY

Mrs. Morales knew that Julio and Carlos would have to make up before they could celebrate her birthday. That's exactly what she wanted. She could not understand how two brothers could let a silly argument keep them apart for so long. They would have to learn to forgive each other.

Jesus told his friends that forgiveness is an important part of preparing for worship.

If you bring your gift to the altar, and there recall that your brother or sister has anything against you, leave your gift there at the altar, go first and be reconciled with your brother or sister, and then come and offer your gift.

MATTHEW 5:23–24

Just as their mother's party gave Julio and Carlos an opportunity to forgive each other, Catholics have the opportunity to seek forgiveness at the beginning of every Mass.

In the Penitential Rite, you admit that you have sinned and pray for God's forgiveness. You ask for God's forgiveness using either the "Lord, Have Mercy" litany or the "I Confess." Sometimes the priest sprinkles you with holy water as a sign of God's forgiveness.

Except during Lent, the Gloria—a song of praise to God—is sung following the Penitential Rite. The Gloria is followed by the Opening Prayer. This is a prayer said by the priest. He invites you to turn your thoughts to God by saying, "Let us pray."

YOU'RE INVITED

Lucia and her mother sent invitations to all of the members of the Morales family so that they would know where and when to gather to celebrate Mrs. Morales' birthday. Make an invitation for your parish family, inviting them to Sunday Mass. Be sure to mention the time and place and to tell what is being celebrated.

WORDS OF WELCOME

The prayers of the Mass are often taken directly from the Bible. These prayers help the Christian family praise and thank God. The celebrant's words of greeting at Mass are based on Saint Paul's letter to the Christian community at Corinth.

One form of the greeting is printed here with words missing. If you need help filling in the missing words, look up the very last sentence of Saint Paul's Second Letter to the Corinthians.

"The _____ of our Lord Jesus _____ and the _____ of _____ and the _____ of the _____ Spirit be with _you_ all."

THE PEOPLE'S WORK

When Catholics gather to worship in public, they are celebrating liturgy. The word *liturgy* comes from the Greek word meaning "the work of God's people." What is the work you do at Mass?

When Jesus and his disciples finished the Last Supper, they stood with their hands turned to heaven and sang the traditional Passover psalms *(Matthew 26:30)*. By his own example, Jesus taught that liturgical prayer goes beyond words and thoughts. In the liturgy, you pray with your body as well as with words. What are some of the gestures you use during the Mass?

_____

_____

_____

_____

_____

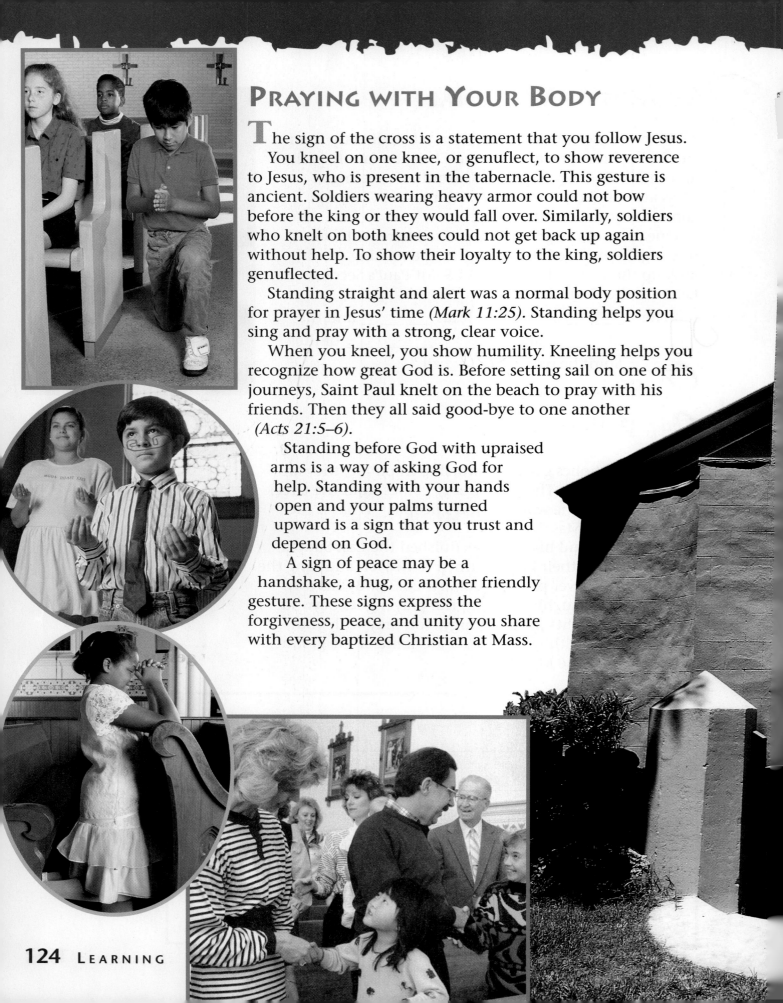

PRAYING WITH YOUR BODY

The sign of the cross is a statement that you follow Jesus.

You kneel on one knee, or genuflect, to show reverence to Jesus, who is present in the tabernacle. This gesture is ancient. Soldiers wearing heavy armor could not bow before the king or they would fall over. Similarly, soldiers who knelt on both knees could not get back up again without help. To show their loyalty to the king, soldiers genuflected.

Standing straight and alert was a normal body position for prayer in Jesus' time *(Mark 11:25)*. Standing helps you sing and pray with a strong, clear voice.

When you kneel, you show humility. Kneeling helps you recognize how great God is. Before setting sail on one of his journeys, Saint Paul knelt on the beach to pray with his friends. Then they all said good-bye to one another *(Acts 21:5–6)*.

Standing before God with upraised arms is a way of asking God for help. Standing with your hands open and your palms turned upward is a sign that you trust and depend on God.

A sign of peace may be a handshake, a hug, or another friendly gesture. These signs express the forgiveness, peace, and unity you share with every baptized Christian at Mass.

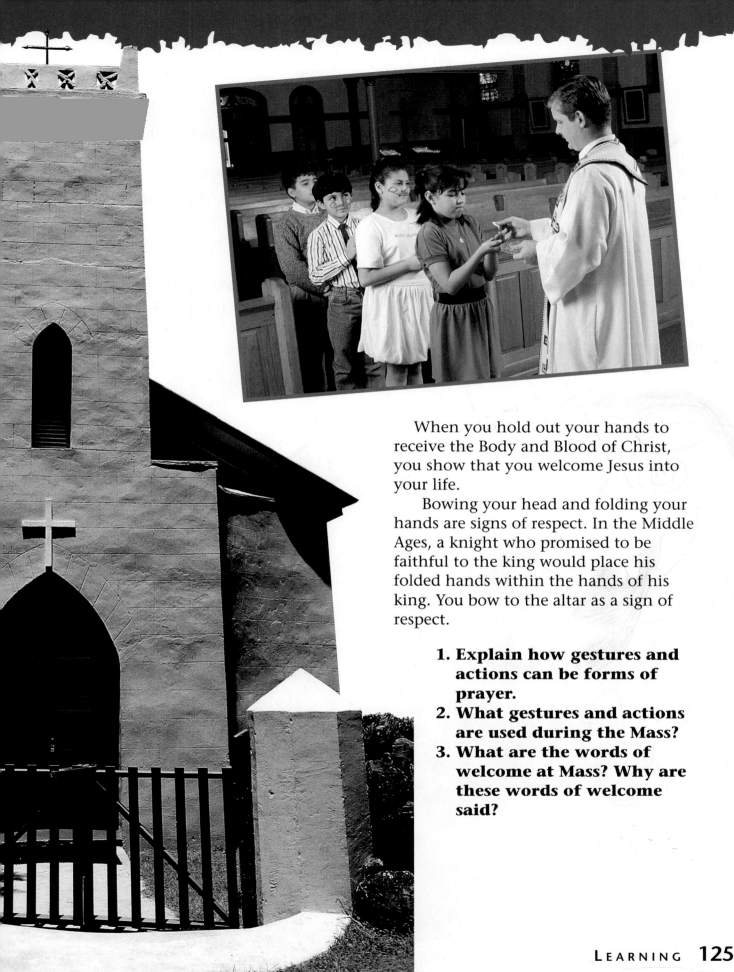

When you hold out your hands to receive the Body and Blood of Christ, you show that you welcome Jesus into your life.

Bowing your head and folding your hands are signs of respect. In the Middle Ages, a knight who promised to be faithful to the king would place his folded hands within the hands of his king. You bow to the altar as a sign of respect.

1. **Explain how gestures and actions can be forms of prayer.**
2. **What gestures and actions are used during the Mass?**
3. **What are the words of welcome at Mass? Why are these words of welcome said?**

WORDS OF PRAISE

Catholics gather at Mass to offer praise and thanks to God. The Glory to God is one of the Church's oldest prayers of praise. Pray or sing this ancient canticle while standing. The early Christians stood when they praised God.

Glory to God in the highest, and peace to his people on earth.

Lord God, heavenly king, almighty God and Father,

we worship you, we give you thanks,

we praise you for your glory.

Lord Jesus Christ, only Son of the Father,

Lord God, Lamb of God, you take away the sin of the world:

have mercy on us;

you are seated at the right hand of the Father: receive our prayer.

For you alone are the Holy One, you alone are the Lord,

you alone are the Most High, Jesus Christ,

with the Holy Spirit, in the glory of God the Father.

Amen.

WITH YOUR FAMILY

What does your family do to welcome new people into your neighborhood or community? Discuss with your family ways that you can make other people feel they belong. Decide on one thing that you can do as a family to make other people feel welcome at church.

▼ REVIEW CHAPTER 14 ....

CATHOLICS BELIEVE

1. The Catholic family gathers at Mass.
2. The Introductory Rites at Mass are the procession, the greeting, the Penitential Rite, the Gloria, and the opening prayer.

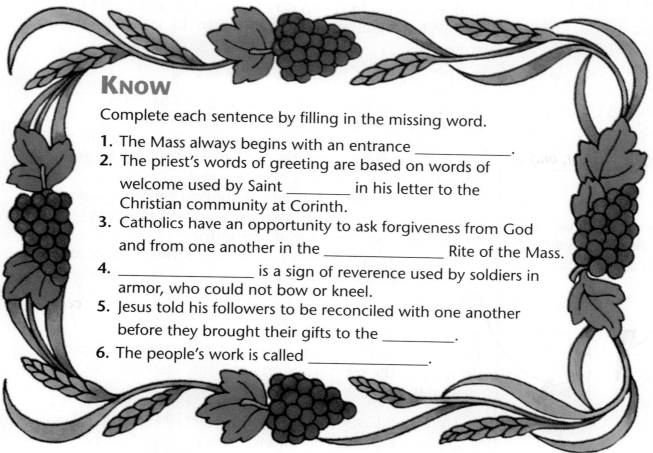

KNOW

Complete each sentence by filling in the missing word.

1. The Mass always begins with an entrance _____.
2. The priest's words of greeting are based on words of welcome used by Saint _____ in his letter to the Christian community at Corinth.
3. Catholics have an opportunity to ask forgiveness from God and from one another in the _____ Rite of the Mass.
4. _____ is a sign of reverence used by soldiers in armor, who could not bow or kneel.
5. Jesus told his followers to be reconciled with one another before they brought their gifts to the _____.
6. The people's work is called _____.

SUNDAY MASS

The Mass is the prayer of the whole community, not just the prayer of the celebrant, the lector, or the choir. All the people present are asked to join their voices together in prayer. When all of the voices are joined, the church is filled with sound. Each individual's voice and prayer becomes part of the mosaic of prayer.

At Mass this Sunday, listen to the sounds of the community at prayer. Then add your voice to the community's prayer. If you are not sure about the words, use a missalette to help you.

15

Let the word of Christ dwell in you richly.

COLOSSIANS 3:16

CONTENT KEYS

1. God is revealed in Scripture.
2. The Liturgy of the Word reveals God at Mass.
3. The Word of God is present among the people.

Write in the space some other examples that show the power of words.

THE POWER OF A WORD

Words have power. What do you feel when someone makes you a promise, thanks you for doing something kind, or shouts, "You can do it!" when it's your turn to play? What is the power of the word in the following stories?

MESSED-UP MORNING

Adrian was having a terrible morning. His hair was sticking up on one side, he couldn't find his favorite shoes, and he missed the bus. To top it off, Adrian didn't remember that his oral book report was due until he got to school. "Oh no, not today!" he groaned.

Overhearing his words, Mrs. Robinson smiled. Speaking softly, she said to Adrian, "I know you'll do a fine job. Please have your report ready tomorrow."

Adrian couldn't believe his ears. He began to smile as he looked up at Mrs. Robinson. Maybe his day wouldn't be so bad after all.

JUST A NOTE

Elena's old chocolate box was filled with treasures. Right on top was the postcard from her Nana. Elena read it every day.

My dearest Elena. Just a little note to let you know that I am well. I am enjoying my visit with Uncle Rudy, but I miss you very much. I'll be home soon. I can't wait to tell you about my trip. Love and hugs. Nana.

Elena smiled as she hugged the postcard. Reading it made her feel as if her grandmother were already with her. Elena tucked the postcard back into her box. She would read it again later.

In a Whisper

The prophet Elijah was in trouble. Queen Jezebel wanted to kill him. An angel of God warned Elijah to flee from the queen's wrath. Elijah escaped to the mountain of God, Horeb.

While on the mountain, Elijah listened for direction from God. He felt a wind strong enough to crush stone, but God was not in the wind. After the wind, Elijah felt a strong earthquake, but God was not there either. Then there came a blazing fire, but God was not in the fire. Finally Elijah heard a tiny whispering sound. And that is where he found God.

Based on 1 KINGS 19:1–13

The Power of God's Word

You know that some words are filled with power. The words "good job" or "I appreciate everything you do" can change the way you feel and think. Other words can have a negative power. Having someone say "you're no good" or "you're stupid" can ruin your whole day. Sometimes words can bore you or put you to sleep.

Unlike the words you hear all day from the radio or TV, God's words are always filled with power, even when they are spoken only in the slightest whisper. After listening to God on Mount Horeb, Elijah stopped being afraid. He returned to Israel and continued to preach about the evils of the queen. Another example of the power of God's words can be found in the story of creation in Genesis. God creates the heavens, the earth, and everything on the earth simply by saying "Let it be."

God's word is not only powerful. It is also surprising. As Elijah found out, God's word comes when it is least expected, often in an unusual way. Saint Augustine learned firsthand about the power and surprising nature of God's word. Because of God's word, Augustine's whole life was changed.

BREAKING THE CHAINS

Augustine had learned about God as a child. Augustine's mother, Monica, sent him to religion classes. She shared her faith with him. But Augustine cared nothing about God. He was more interested in scholarly arguments, gambling, and living a wild life.

When he was 32, Augustine began to have doubts about his life and values. He was not happy. He had hurt too many people and did not know how to say, "I'm sorry." Augustine later wrote that he felt like he was living in chains he couldn't break. Augustine prayed, "How long, O Lord, do I have to wait? How long are you going to leave me in my sins?"

Augustine's prayer was answered immediately. He heard a gentle, childlike voice say, "Take up and read." Augustine jumped to his feet, ran to where his friend Alipius sat, and took the scroll Alipius was reading.

It is now the hour for you to awake from sleep. For our salvation is nearer at hand than we first believed; the night is advanced, the day is at hand. Let us then throw off the works of darkness and put on the armor of light.

ROMANS 13:11–12

Augustine's life was changed by that reading. He began to pray and to study the Scriptures. He changed the way he lived and began to act as a Christian. Six months later, he was baptized. He became a priest four years later, and eventually he was named a bishop. The story of Saint Augustine's life, found in his book, *The Confessions*, has helped many people come to know Jesus.

Listen to God's Word

READ EACH SCRIPTURE PASSAGE. WHAT DOES EACH TELL YOU ABOUT THE POWER OF GOD'S WORD?

JOHN 6:68–69

MATTHEW 7:21

JAMES 1:22–24

HEBREWS 4:12

JOHN 1:14

WORDS OF LIFE

Saint Paul traveled to many different cities to teach about Jesus and share God's word. God's word through Paul was very powerful.

Scene 1: A bakery in first century Greece. A 12-year-old boy is sweeping the floor.

Baker: Why are you in such a hurry to clean up tonight, Eutychus?

Eutychus: The missionary Paul is coming to celebrate the Lord's Supper with us. If I get there early, I can sit by the window, where it is cool.

Baker: I'll give you some bread to take with you to share.

Scene 2: A dining room in a Greek home. People are sitting around the table listening to Paul speak. Eutychus is sitting on a wide window ledge.

Saint Paul: Tomorrow I must leave Troas and move on. But tonight I have so much to tell you.

Narrator: Paul spoke long into the night telling people the wonderful news about Jesus. Eutychus became wrapped up in Paul's words. After a while, he forgot where he was. Leaning back, he fell out of the window.

A Man: Paul! Eutychus has fallen! Help us!

A Woman: He's not moving. Is he dead?

Narrator: Everyone ran outside to help Eutychus. Paul bent down and lifted Eutychus off of the ground.

Paul: Don't be alarmed. There's life in him. Let us ask Jesus to heal him.

Eutychus: What happened? Why am I here?

Paul: Give praise to God!

(Everybody hugs Paul and Eutychus)

Paul: When Christ was raised from the dead, he destroyed our last enemy, death itself. So even though we all die, we will all be brought to life again in Christ.

Based on Acts 20:7–12

The Next Morning

Write an ending to the play. What might Eutychus say to the baker the next morning?

God's Word in Scripture

Eutychus was held spellbound by the power of Saint Paul's words. Think about what it would have been like to learn about Jesus directly from one of the Apostles. You can no longer learn about Jesus from Saint Paul himself, but you can learn about God the Father and Jesus from reading the Bible.

God is always speaking to the world, telling about the love of the Trinity. God's act of speaking is known as God's revelation. The story of God's revelation to the Hebrew people is found in the forty-six books of the Hebrew Scriptures, the Old Testament. The story of God's revelation through Jesus and the Holy Spirit is found in the twenty-seven books of the Christian Scriptures, or the New Testament. These seventy-three books combined are known as the Bible, or Sacred Scriptures.

Christians believe that God is revealed through the stories and prayers in the Bible. The Sacred Scriptures are honored in a special way by Christians. Followers of Jesus are nourished and strengthened by God's Word in Scripture. They read from the Bible as part of their personal prayer.

Reading from the Bible is also part of every act of Catholic worship. When you celebrate a sacrament, you will hear at least one reading from the Bible. Many of the prayers Catholics pray come directly from the Bible. The greatest of all prayers, the Eucharist, comes from the Bible. In fact, one of the major parts of the Liturgy of the Eucharist is called the Liturgy of the Word.

THE LITURGY OF THE WORD

The first reading at Mass is taken from the Old Testament. You hear stories of God's loving relationship with Israel. These are the same Scriptures that Jesus heard in the Jewish synagogue services. After the reading, the lector says, "The Word of the Lord." You respond "Thanks be to God."

After the first reading, the Responsorial Psalm is sung. This is a hymn of praise taken from the Hebrew Scriptures.

The second reading is usually taken from the letters of Saint Paul or of other leaders of the early Church. These letters or epistles, were originally written to Christians who wanted to learn more about Jesus. After this reading, the lector once again says, "The Word of the Lord," and again you respond, "Thanks be to God."

The most important reading at Mass is the Gospel. The Gospel tells about the life and teaching of Jesus. Before the Gospel reading, the people stand to sing the Gospel acclamation, "Alleluia," which means "Praise the Lord!" After the Gospel, the priest or deacon says, "The Gospel of the Lord." You respond by saying, "Praise to you Lord Jesus Christ."

In the homily, the brief talk that follows the Gospel reading, the priest or

deacon applies the reading to modern situations. The homily helps you to understand God's word and put it into practice in your life.

The Liturgy of the Word continues after the homily with the proclamation of the Creed. The Liturgy of the Word ends with the Prayer of the Faithful, or General Intercessions. In these prayers, the needs of the Church community around the world are offered to God. The special needs of your parish are also prayed for at this time.

1. **What are the parts of the Liturgy of the Word?**
2. **Look in a Bible. Who wrote the New Testament letters? To whom were the letters written?**
3. **What is the purpose of the homily?**

At dinner each night this week, take turns reading short passages from the Bible with your family. Talk about the message God is giving to your family.

RESPONDING TO GOD'S WORD

Jesus told his followers to "hear the word of God and to act on it" *(Luke 8:21)*. Each of the messages below comes from the Word of God. Tell how you can respond to each message.

"Be generous to all the living"
(Sirach 7:33).

_____

_____

_____

"This is my commandment: love one another as I love you" (John 15:12).

_____

_____

_____

"Welcome one another, then, as Christ welcomed you, for the glory of God" (Romans 15:7).

_____

_____

_____

CELEBRATING GOD'S WORD

Celebrate a Liturgy of the Word with your classmates or family.

Reading: *Isaiah 55:10–11*

Response: *The seed that falls on good ground will produce a rich harvest.*

Reading: *1 Corinthians 13:4–7*

Acclamation: *Alleluia, alleluia! The seed is the Word of God, Christ is the sower; all who come to him will live forever. Alleluia!*

Gospel: *Matthew 13:1–9*

Response: *Praise to you, Lord Jesus Christ.*

FOLLOWING Jesus

There are a few simple things you can do to make the readings at the Sunday liturgy more meaningful. Read the readings from Scripture in advance. Think about what they say to you. Pick out one phrase to carry with you. Develop your own homily. What would you say to other people about the reading? Compare your homily to the one given by the priest.

CATHOLICS BELIEVE

1. God is revealed, or speaks to you, in Scripture.
2. At Mass, you share God's Word in the Liturgy of the Word.

KNOW

Complete each sentence by choosing the right word from within the parentheses.

1. The Liturgy of the Word is the part of the Mass that shares (the Scriptures, Holy Communion).
2. The letters of Saint Paul are collected in the (New Testament, Old Testament).
3. Between the first and second readings, you say or sing a responsorial (psalm, acclamation).
4. The priest or deacon gives a (homily, hymn) to help the people understand God's Word.
5. The Gospel Acclamation "Alleluia!" means ("Amen," "Praise the Lord").

SUNDAY MASS

Read the Gospel for this Sunday. Your teacher will help you find it. Pick one phrase from this reading to think about before Sunday. What would you say in a homily about this reading?

SEASONAL MISSALETTE
ORDINARY TIME

I tend my sheep

Do this in memory of me.

LUKE 22:19

A MEAL TO REMEMBER

CONTENT KEYS

1. **Eucharist is a Greek word that means "gratitude."**
2. **The Eucharistic Banquet is a sacrificial meal.**
3. **Jesus Christ is truly present in the Eucharist.**

I went with my friend Ella to her grandmother's house to celebrate the feast of Passover. Passover is a very important day for Jews.

Ella spread a sparkling white cloth on the dining room table, and I put new candles in the gleaming silver candlesticks. Ella's brothers, Daniel and Michael, set wine glasses for everyone and placed a special goblet, called the cup of Elijah, in the middle of the table. Ella then brought in the silver tray with the matzoh, the flat, unleavened bread eaten at Passover. The bread is flat because it is made without yeast.

When we were all gathered around the table, Ella's grandmother lighted the candles and said a blessing prayer. Then Ella's father rose and announced, "Tonight we celebrate the Passover, the feast of freedom and redemption. We remember our history. We begin the Haggadah." Ella whispered to me that "Haggadah" means "the telling of a story."

Because he is the youngest, Daniel asked, "Why is this night different from all other nights?"

"That's how we introduce the Passover story," Ella whispered again. Her father answered each question Daniel asked with a story about what God had done for the people of Israel.

The Passover meal was different from other meals. We tasted special foods. We sang a thanksgiving song about God's blessings. And when the wine was blessed, I got to drink a little sip.

Celebrating Passover helped me understand a little better what it means to be Jewish. Passover also helped me understand better what it means to be Catholic.

1. **How do Ella and her family celebrate Passover?**
2. **What are some of the things about the Passover meal that remind you of the Eucharist?**

THE PASSOVER STORY

Passover celebrates the time when God freed the Chosen People from slavery in Egypt. The story of Passover is important to Jews and Christians alike.

Moses stood before the people. They were tired and dusty after their long day working as slaves in the Egyptian brickyards.

"The time has come," Moses said quietly, but with an unmistakable urgency in his voice. "God has heard your cries for help. Tonight we will leave this land, and not even Pharaoh will be able to stop us."

The people listened intently.

"You must do exactly as I say," Moses continued. "Your lives depend on it.

"Every family must sacrifice a lamb," Moses directed them. "Mark your doorposts with the lamb's blood. Then get ready for a journey. Do not wait for the dough for your bread to rise. Eat the roasted lamb with some bitter herbs and the unleavened bread. Eat standing up, with sandals on your feet and your staff in hand, ready to flee. And remember that God is with you."

"How will this make Pharaoh give us our freedom?" the people asked, because it was almost too much to hope for.

"Tonight," Moses explained, "the Angel of Death will pass over Egypt. Death will strike the firstborn of every Egyptian family—even the family of the Pharaoh. But God's angel will see the blood of the lamb on your doorposts and will pass over your houses."

Based on EXODUS 12:1–13

KEEP THIS FEAST

Everything happened just as Moses said it would. The people of Israel left the land of Egypt, passing through the Red Sea into freedom. After many years in the desert they entered the Promised Land. Since that time, the Jewish people have celebrated the feast of Passover. They celebrate that God saved them from slavery. They celebrate that God led them to freedom. They celebrate that God gave them a home. They celebrate that God made them the Chosen People.

Moses instructed the Jewish people to remember God's saving acts, saying:

Keep, then, this feast of the unleavened bread. Observe this rite when you have entered the land which the Lord has promised you. When your children ask you, "What does this rite mean?" you shall reply, "This is the Passover sacrifice of the Lord, who passed over the houses of the Israelites in Egypt, striking down the Egyptians, and sparing our houses."

EXODUS 12:17, 24–27

At the Passover meal, Jews eat these special foods.

- *matzoh,* to remember the rushed journey from slavery
- *haroset,* a mixture of chopped nuts, apples, and cinnamon to remember the mortar the Israelites made as slaves
- *bitter herbs,* such as horseradish and radishes, to remember the bitterness of slavery

- *roasted lamb bone,* to remember the Paschal lamb
- *eggs,* to remember the offering that accompanied the sacrifice of the Paschal lamb at the Temple at Jerusalem
- *salt or salt water,* to remember the tears the Israelites cried while in slavery
- *tender green vegetables,* to remember that God gave them a new life

1. **What is the meaning of the Passover feast?**
2. **What are some reasons why Passover is important to Catholics?**

CELEBRATING EUCHARIST

Peter and John paused near a wall overlooking the courtyard, amazed at the huge crowd of people filling the streets below.

"Peter, what do you see when you look at these people?" asked John.

"I see the whole people of Israel returning to Jerusalem for Passover, just as we have," replied Peter.

"Look deeper," urged John. "Think like Jesus."

Puzzled, Peter looked again. "Ah," he marveled. "I see a brother or sister in every face. They are our brothers and sisters because God led our ancestors out of slavery in Egypt. Tonight we will once again share the unleavened bread just as our ancestors did in Egypt."

"And we will all share the Passover cup as we ask God to send the Messiah," added John.

"You understand so well," said Jesus, startling his disciples. "That's why I want to eat this Passover meal with my friends. Go now to the upper room and prepare the Passover meal. Tonight is the night."

As the disciples disappeared into the crowd, Jesus thought to himself, "This Passover, we will do more than remember. Tonight, freedom from slavery will become freedom from sin and death. Tonight, the unleavened bread that was food for the desert will become food for eternal life. And tonight, the wine of joyful hope will be my life's blood poured out for the life of the world. After tonight, they will celebrate a new Passover to remember my sacrifice."

In My Memory

Just as Moses told the people how the Passover feast should be celebrated, Jesus told his followers how they were to remember his sacrifice with a meal. Saint Paul gave these same instructions to the Christian community he started in Corinth.

> *The Lord Jesus, on the night he was handed over, took bread, and after he had given thanks, broke it and said, "This is my body that is for you. Do this in remembrance of me." In the same way also the cup, after supper, saying, "This is the **new covenant** in my blood. Do this, as often as you drink it, in remembrance of me." For as often as you eat this bread and drink the cup, you proclaim the death of the Lord until he comes.*
>
> 1 Corinthians 11:23–26

In the Eucharist, Jesus is remembered. The sacrifice that Jesus offered with his death on Calvary is made present and real once again. You are invited to join Jesus in the offering of himself to God. You can take your daily life, with its joys and sorrows, and unite them with the love of Jesus. The bread and wine actually become Jesus' Body and Blood. This is called the Real Presence. And as you receive Jesus, you become more like him. The Eucharist is always a celebration of praise and thanks to God for the saving action of Jesus.

Remember Me

Find five things in the quotation from 1 Corinthians 11:23–26 that Jesus told his followers to do in order to remember his sacrifice.

1.   4.

2.   5.

3.

SPECIAL WORDS

In the old covenant, God promises the people of Israel a Promised Land if they keep God's commandments. In the **new covenant,** God promises eternal life to those who love Jesus and follow his teachings.

THE LITURGY OF THE EUCHARIST

There are five major parts in the Liturgy of the Eucharist: the Presentation of the Gifts, the Preface, the Eucharistic Prayer, the Memorial Acclamation, and the Great Amen.

PRESENTATION OF THE GIFTS

Following the Prayers of the Faithful, the gifts of bread and wine are brought to the altar. The priest blesses these gifts using the ancient prayers of blessing offered by Jewish people on the Sabbath, "Blessed are you, Lord God of all creation. Through your goodness we have bread to offer." After each blessing you respond, "Blessed be God forever."

PREFACE

The Eucharistic Prayer begins with the Preface. The Church gives thanks to the the Father, the Son, and the Holy Spirit for creating the world and for sending Jesus to save all people. The preface ends with a hymn of praise called the *Sanctus*, meaning "holy."

EUCHARISTIC PRAYER

The priest prays that you and everyone at the Eucharist become one body and one spirit in Christ. Then, following Jesus' instructions at the Last Supper, the priest says the words of Jesus over the bread and wine. The bread and wine become the Body and Blood of Christ. The sacrifice Jesus offered on the cross is made present.

MEMORIAL ACCLAMATION

The priest says, "Let us proclaim the mystery of faith." You respond with the Memorial Acclamation. The acclamation states your belief in the saving death and resurrection of Jesus. The most common response is "Christ has died, Christ is risen, Christ will come again!"

GREAT AMEN

At the end of the Eucharistic Prayer, you proclaim your union with Christ's sacrifice by saying or singing the word "Amen."

1. **What does it mean to say that the Mass is a meal?**
2. **What is remembered at Mass?**
3. **What happens at Mass to make it more than just a remembrance of Jesus?**

Following Jesus

Jesus thanked his Father for the bread and wine he was about to share with his friends. Saying thanks to God and to others is a good way to follow Jesus. Write a thank-you note to someone who has helped you or given you something. Remember that person in your prayers at Mass.

PRAISE AND THANKS

When you remember God's work of salvation, you want to shout praise to God. When you remember the blessings God has given you, you want to give thanks. Finish each of the following statements. Then give thanks to God by saying the prayer of praise.

I am thankful for my family because

_____

I am thankful for my friends because

_____

I am thankful for my Catholic faith because

_____

I am thankful for God's gift of

_____

I will show my gratitude by

_____

PRAYER OF PRAISE

Group 1: *Father, all-powerful and ever-living God, we do well always and everywhere to give you thanks.*

Group 2: *With the choirs of angels in heaven we proclaim your glory and join in their unending hymn of praise:*

> **Group 1:** *Holy, holy, holy Lord, God of power and might, heaven and earth are full of your glory. Hosanna in the highest.*

> **Group 2:** *Blessed is he who comes in the name of the Lord. Hosanna in the highest.*

▼REVIEW CHAPTER 16

CATHOLICS BELIEVE

1. In the Liturgy of the Eucharist, you remember and give thanks to God for Jesus' death and resurrection.
2. The Eucharist is both a sacrifice and a meal.
3. In the Eucharist, bread and wine become the Body and Blood of Christ.

KNOW

Use the clues to help you solve the crossword puzzle.

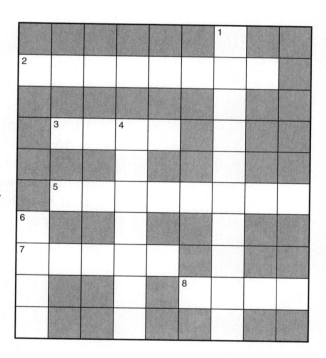

Down

1. The kind of bread used for the Eucharist.

4. "Let us proclaim the _____ of faith."

6. The Eucharistic Prayer ends with the great _____.

Across

2. Jesus made a new _____ with his followers.

3. The Israelites marked their doorposts with the blood of the _____.

5. The Jewish feast celebrating God's saving power.

7. _____ led the Israelites out of Egypt.

8. The Mass is a holy _____ that remembers Jesus' sacrifice.

SUNDAY MASS

Read the four statements of faith commonly said at the Memorial Acclamation. Your teacher will help you find them in the Mass book. With a friend, practice remembering them. See how quickly you can learn the acclamations.

SHARE

CONTENT KEYS

1. **Jesus gives himself as bread and wine.**
2. **The risen Jesus gives peace.**
3. **You are united with the risen Jesus at communion.**

Let the peace of Christ live in your hearts, the peace into which you were called in one body.

From COLOSSIANS 3:15

THE HEAVENLY BANQUET

Old Tan entered the great banquet hall of heaven. Gorgeous silk screens decorated the room and a long table stretched down the center of the hall. The table was set with bowls of pearly rice, tantalizing crabcakes, luscious steamed shrimp, juicy fruits, and tempting sweets.

Tan was very hungry. There were many other people already seated at the table, but Tan easily found a place to sit. On the table in front of him he found a pair of very long chopsticks. Tan could pick up food with the chopsticks, but he could not feed himself with them, no matter what he tried.

Then Tan had an idea. He picked up a bite of rice with his chopsticks and reached across the table, offering the rice to the child seated there. The hungry child opened her mouth happily and ate the rice. Then she fed Tan.

Here was the solution! When people saw Tan and the young girl feeding each other, they did the same. Some people, however, became so annoyed with the chopsticks that they left the table grumbling angrily, and went away lonely and hungry.

Based on a Vietnamese folktale

The Hungry Heart

People are hungry for more than food. Look at the list of different kinds of hungers. What could you do to satisfy each of these hungers?

Hunger	Nourishment
Empty stomach	
Lonely heart	
Sad spirit	
Anxious mind	
Hurt feelings	
Bored brain	

BREAD FROM HEAVEN

We were up early that morning, searching for Jesus of Nazareth. The day before, he had fed all of us—thousands of us!—with only a few loaves of bread and a couple of fish. He had slipped away quietly afterward, going off alone to pray. When the sun's rays were just touching the ripples on the Sea of Galilee, we found him again on the other shore.

I'm not sure why the others were there, but I was still hungry. Not for bread or fish, but for the warm sound of his voice. I was hungry for teachings I had never heard before. I was hungry for the feeling of being one of his disciples. Some people in the crowd, though, were just hungry for miracles.

"Show us a sign!" they cried out to Jesus. "Our ancestors ate manna in the desert. "What will you give us?" they demanded now.

"I am the Bread of Life," Jesus said quietly. "Whoever comes to me will never hunger, and whoever believes in me will never thirst."

Some of the people who heard this began to laugh.

Jesus continued, "Your ancestors ate manna in the desert, but they died. I am the living Bread that came down from heaven; whoever eats this Bread will live forever; and the Bread that I will give is my flesh for the life of the world."

I didn't understand then what he meant. But I knew that I wanted to learn more from Jesus. From that day on, I followed Jesus of Nazareth. And even now, when we gather to remember him in the Lord's Supper, his words fill my heart.

Based on JOHN 6:30–31, 47–51

TAKE AND EAT

Jesus knew that after he returned to his Father, his followers would continue to hunger for his voice, his touch, his words, and his presence. At the last supper he ate with his friends, Jesus gave himself as bread to eat. "Take and eat," he said to them. "This is my body."

In the Eucharist, you share the Bread of Life with all those who gather at the Table of the Lord. The gifts of bread and wine are changed into the Body and Blood of Jesus by the power of the Holy Spirit. They still look and taste like bread and wine, but they have truly become the risen Lord.

Jesus did not leave you to starve on your journey through life. In the Eucharist, Jesus is with you every step of the way.

1. **What did God feed the Israelites in the desert?**
2. **What did Jesus feed the hungry crowd on the seashore?**
3. **In what ways does Jesus still feed people today?**

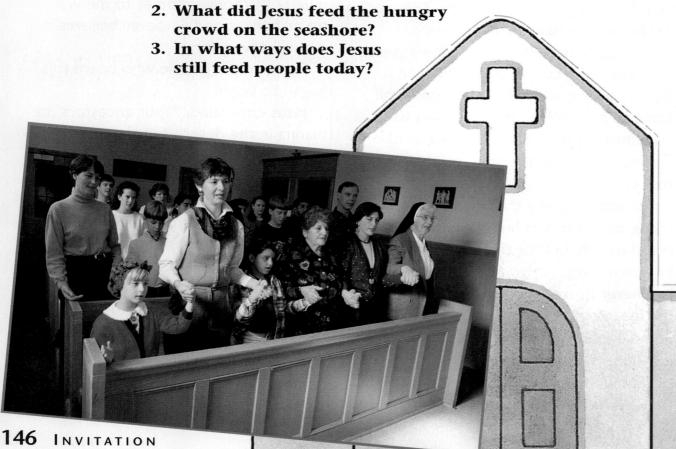

THE PEACE OF CHRIST

Along with his presence in the Eucharist, Jesus gave his friends another great gift—the gift of peace. "Peace I leave with you; my peace I give to you. Do not let your hearts be troubled or afraid" *(John 14:27)*. The peace of Christ is a blessing that comes with being one with Jesus. Like food, it is a gift that God gives for you to share.

The Communion Rite of the Mass, which incudes all the prayers and actions between the Great Amen and the final blessing, is the time when you share both the Bread of Life and the peace of Christ with others. Each of the prayers and actions of the Communion rite is a sign of unity between Jesus and his followers.

COMING IN PEACE

The Communion Rite begins with the Lord's Prayer. In this prayer, which Jesus gave to his followers, you ask God the Father to provide you with what you need.

- When you share the sign of peace, you show that you are at peace not only with your family and others at Mass, but with all people everywhere.
- Jesus is the Lamb of God who brings peace by taking away sin. You ask Jesus for his mercy and peace.

Before Communion, the ancient words of a Roman soldier are offered as a sign of faith. The centurion asked Jesus to heal his dying servant. The centurion said that he was not worthy for Jesus to come to his house. Recognizing Jesus' authority, the centurion added, "Say the word and my servant will be healed." Amazed by the soldier's faith, Jesus healed the servant from afar (*Luke 7:6–10*).

- The priest invites you to come to the table of the Lord. Your "Amen" says that you believe that you are receiving the Body and Blood of Jesus. Every time you receive the Body of Christ, you grow closer to Jesus and to all Christians, so that together you become the Body of Christ.

- After Communion, the priest and people pray silently for a while. Then the priest says a prayer that concludes the Communion Rite. The Prayer after Communion changes each Sunday, according to the feast or liturgical season.

FOLLOWING Jesus

Being a peacemaker means being a person who brings the gift of God's peace to others. Peacemakers smooth troubled feelings. They also try to find out what is churning up the feelings in the first place. Here are three things you can do to become a peacemaker:

1. Try to understand why you or others are angry or upset.
2. Try to solve the problem or change the situation.
3. Stay calm. Don't let other people's anger make you angry.

BLESSED ARE THE PEACEMAKERS

The peace of Christ doesn't happen just in church. The world is hungry for his peace. Read about three people who could be peacemakers. Tell how each can bring peace to the situation.

MEET BRET

Bret waited 45 minutes for a ride home after basketball practice. Bret was really upset because his dad was so late. When his dad finally picked Bret up, Bret did not even give his dad a chance to explain. Bret sulked and refused to talk to his dad during the 10-minute ride home.

How can Bret be a peacemaker?

_____

_____

MEET KENDRA

Carla balanced her food tray as she scanned the cafeteria looking for a good place to sit. "Is this place open?" she asked a group of girls in her class.

"No," Jackie answered quickly. "We're saving it for someone."

Kendra, who was sitting at the table, knew this wasn't true. When she saw Carla sitting alone, Kendra didn't feel good about what Jackie had done.

How can Kendra be a peacemaker?

_____

_____

MEET PETER

Peter finished doing a math problem on the board. Mrs. Maccini thanked him for having done a great job. As Peter was returning to his desk, Dion put his foot out in the aisle and Peter stumbled over it. Peter knew he had been tripped on purpose, but Dion said innocently, "Sorry, it was an accident."

How can Peter be a peacemaker?

_____

_____

1. **Describe the kind of peace that Jesus wishes to give you in Communion.**
2. **Explain why the Church uses the sign of peace in the Communion Rite.**

THE PRAYER OF SAINT FRANCIS

When Francis was a boy, he was rich. He had a big allowance, the coolest clothes, his own horse. He had everything that money could buy. But Francis was hungry for friendship with Jesus. When he got older, Francis followed Jesus with his whole heart. Then Francis became rich in the peace of Christ.

Francis was so full of peace and joy that many people came to him to learn his secret. One thing about real peace is that you can't keep it for yourself. You have to share it. The prayer of Saint Francis can help you learn how to share the peace of Christ.

*Lord, make me an instrument
of your peace;
where there is hatred, let me sow love;
where there is injury, pardon;
where there is doubt, faith;
   where there is despair, hope;
     where there is darkness, light;
       and where there is sadness, joy.
        O Divine Master,
         grant that I may not so much
          seek to be consoled as to console;
           to be understood as to understand;
         to be loved as to love;
       for it is in giving that we receive;
it is in pardoning that we are pardoned;
and it is in dying that we are born
to eternal life.*

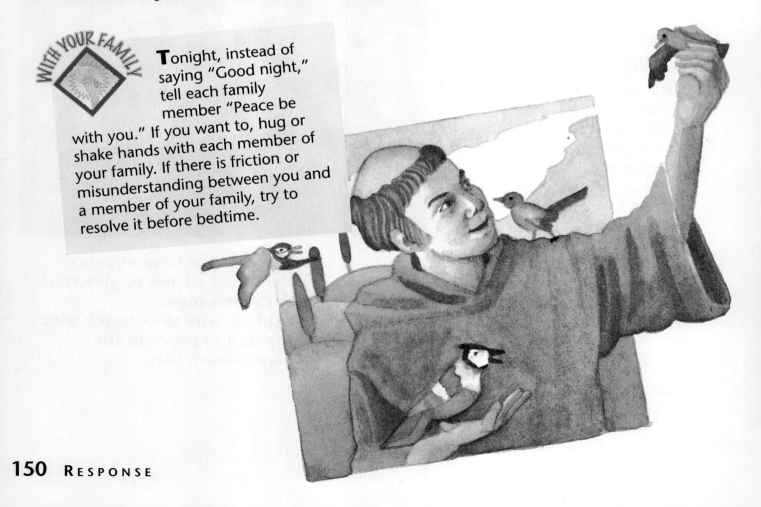

WITH YOUR FAMILY

Tonight, instead of saying "Good night," tell each family member "Peace be with you." If you want to, hug or shake hands with each member of your family. If there is friction or misunderstanding between you and a member of your family, try to resolve it before bedtime.

CATHOLICS BELIEVE

1. Jesus is the Bread of Life.
2. At Communion you share the Body and Blood of the Risen Lord, whose gift to you is peace.

KNOW

Carefully read each of the statements below. Choose the **T** if the statement is true. Choose the **F** if the statement is false.

T F 1. God fed the Israelites with manna in the desert.

T F 2. When Jesus said, "I am the Bread of Life," everyone understood what he meant.

T F 3. In the Eucharist, the gifts of bread and wine are changed into the Body and Blood of Jesus.

T F 4. When the priest or eucharistic minister says, "The Body of Christ," you say, "Peace be with you."

T F 5. The Lord's Prayer is part of the Communion Rite.

SUNDAY MASS

During the sign of peace, members of the Church shake hands or hug each other. This Sunday make an extra effort to shake hands and say "peace be with you" to everyone around you. Go across the aisle. Greet people you do not know.

CONTENT KEYS

1. Jesus is truly present at Mass.
2. You are nourished at the Eucharist.
3. Eucharist sends you out to serve others.

> Jesus sent his disciples ahead in pairs to every town and place he intended to visit.
>
> LUKE 10:1

I AM WITH YOU

Jesus promised that wherever two or three people gathered in his name, he would be there with them (*Matthew 18:20*). Take a walk around this neighborhood. Mark a cross in each place where you think Jesus is present.

ON THE ROAD TO EMMAUS

After Jesus died, his disciples were very frightened. Some hid in Jerusalem. Others left Jerusalem for one of the outlying villages. Two of the disciples experienced something special on the road to Emmaus.

First Reader: Two of the disciples are walking to a village seven miles outside of Jerusalem, talking about the things that had happened since Jesus' crucifixion three days ago.

Disciple: Cleopas, my friend, we've made this journey many times before, but it has never felt so long.

Cleopas: I know, it seems to go on forever. It has got to be the longest trip I have ever taken.

Second Reader: As they trudged along, their hearts were heavy with sadness. A voice within them kept saying, "It is over. It is over. No kingdom. No hope. He is gone."

Disciple: Cleopas, you know about what happened Friday? I was thinking about what the soldiers did.

Third Reader: They tried to talk about Jesus, but their pain was too great. When the stranger appeared as if from nowhere, they both jumped.

Stranger: What are you discussing as you walk along?

Disciple: What a question! Where have you been? The whole countryside is talking about how Jesus was crucified. We had hoped that he was the Messiah promised by God. But now he's dead.

Stranger: Such a lot of foolishness! You've read the Scriptures. Why are you so slow to believe them? Isn't this how the Messiah's story is supposed to go?

Fourth Reader: Beginning with Moses and the prophets, the stranger explained what the Scriptures said about the Messiah.

Cleopas: What you say sounds true.

BREAKING BREAD

Fifth Reader: The sun was going down, and it seemed the stranger was about to bid farewell to Cleopas and the other disciple, and go on alone.

Disciple: Please, sir, if you do not have to go on, stay with us. It will soon be dark.

Sixth Reader: Cleopas and the other disciple set a simple supper on the table and asked their guest to pray the mealtime blessing. He took the bread, said the blessing, broke it, and then gave it to Cleopas and the other disciple. At that moment, they saw that the stranger was Jesus. They recognized him in the breaking of the bread. It was exactly what he did at the Last Supper. Then he vanished right before their eyes.

Disciple: I am so happy I don't know whether to laugh or cry.

Cleopas: Didn't your heart burn with joy as you listened to him explain the Scriptures?

Disciple: Jesus really is the Messiah, and he lives. It's not over at all! It's just the beginning.

Cleopas: Let's go to Jerusalem right now and tell the other disciples

what has happened. Let's tell the whole world!

Seventh Reader: The moon was still full. Cleopas and the other disciple could see almost well enough to run. It was the quickest journey they ever took.

Based on LUKE 24:13–35

1. **What helped the disciples recognize Jesus?**
2. **Where do you recognize the presence of Jesus today?**
3. **Which parts of the story remind you of the Mass?**

The Breaking of the Bread

Act out the Emmaus story. How does the breaking of bread remind you of Jesus?

ON THE WAY

Like Cleopas and the other disciple, Christians are on a journey. Each Sunday they stop to rest and gather with other believers who are on the same journey as they are. They gather to hear the word of God broken open and explained. They gather to bless and break the bread that is Jesus. They gather to share the bread that nourishes them and gives them strength to continue on their way. Jesus is present in the Christian assembly, in the word, and in the breaking of the bread.

After Cleopas and the other disciple met Jesus in the word and in the bread, they hurried back to Jerusalem. Nobody told them to go. They wanted to go. They wanted to tell the whole world what had happened to them, how their eyes had been opened. Most of all, they wanted to share the good news of meeting the risen Jesus with their friends in Jerusalem.

Night had fallen by the time their meal with Jesus ended. There was danger of attack by robbers on the dark road back to Jerusalem. But Cleopas and the other disciple were not afraid. This news couldn't wait until morning.

DID YOU KNOW?

When a Catholic near death receives the Eucharist, this last Holy Communion is called *viaticum. Viaticum* is a Latin word that means "something to take with you on the way." Jesus is with his followers on the journey through life and in the final journey through death.

GO FORTH

Every follower of Jesus is called to be an apostle—someone who is sent. Jesus sent his closest friends and helpers, the Apostles, to proclaim the kingdom of God by serving others and by bringing peace to all those they met (see *Matthew 10:5*). Every follower of Jesus has a **mission.** A mission is the work you are sent to do. Your mission is the same as the mission Jesus gave the first Apostles.

YOU ARE SENT

At the end of the Mass, the people are dismissed and given an assignment. Take a closer look at the Concluding Rite of the Mass to see how Christians are sent forth.

The priest says, "The Lord be with you." You answer, "And also with you." This prayer was also used at the beginning of Mass. It is a statement of faith and hope. You believe that Jesus is with you. You trust that Jesus will stay with you.

The priest blesses the people in the name of the Father, and of the Son, and of the Holy Spirit.

The **dismissal** sends forth the people. The priest or deacon chooses from among three options:

"Go in the peace of Christ."

"The Mass is ended, go in peace."

"Go in peace to love and serve the Lord."

SPECIAL WORDS

Look at these words: **Mass, mission, dismissal.** They all come from the Latin word *missa,* which means "to send forth." The Mass prepares Christians for their mission in the world. The dismissal at the end of Mass officially sends them forth on their mission.

FOLLOWING Jesus

Saying a prayer each morning as you begin your day is a good way to remember your mission to do God's work. One very simple morning prayer is based on the prophet Isaiah's answer to God's call: "Here I am, Lord—send me."

Mission Possible

Read each of the passages from Scripture.
Then, in your own words, describe the
mission of a follower of Jesus.

John 20:21

Matthew 28:20

John 14:26

Mark 16:15

Matthew 28:19–20

Matthew 10:32, 39

Ready, Set, Go

Your mission is to love and serve Jesus wherever you find him in the
people of the world. What will you need to help you on this
mission? Look at the packing list below. Check the things you think
you will need.

__ airline tickets

__ hairspray

__ faith

__ cellular phone

__ traveler's checks

__ hope

__ generosity

__ bubblegum

__ extra shoes

__ love

__ freedom

__ courage

__ Bible

__ friends

List two other things you would pack.
Name one talent, skill, or gift that you
could use to carry out your mission.

1. **Jesus' actions at the breaking
   of the bread revealed him to
   the disciples at Emmaus.
   Which of your actions reveal
   that you are a Christian?**
2. **Give an example of a fifth
   grader being an apostle.**
3. **Where did your journey as a
   Christian take you today?**

TO LOVE AND SERVE

You are sent to be an apostle today and every day! You carry out your mission by going to school, playing sports and games, doing your chores, attending church, and hanging out with your friends. Your mission doesn't take you far from home. Your greatest challenge right now may be getting along with your little brother!

Take a look around your own neighborhood. Where do you see Jesus and his followers at work? Where do you see people who need love? Where do you see opportunities to serve?

A mission statement tells how you plan to accomplish your mission. Write your own mission statement here.

_____

_____

_____

A STATEMENT OF PRAISE

John Henry Newman was a scholar, teacher, and priest who lived in England. He wrote about what it means to be sent on a mission by God. Read his statement as your prayer.

"God has created me to do some definite service. God has committed some work to me which he has not committed to any other. I have my mission. I am a link in a chain, a bond of connection between persons. God has not created me for nothing. I shall do good. I shall do God's work. I shall be an angel of peace, a preacher of truth. Whatever, wherever I am, I can never be thrown away. God does nothing in vain. Therefore I shall trust him."

JOHN HENRY NEWMAN (1801–1890)

WITH YOUR FAMILY

When you go home today, be alert. Look for someone who needs your help. Listen for someone who needs to hear an encouraging word. Find a way to offer the help that is needed. Take a moment to give a friend your support.

▼ REVIEW CHAPTER 18 . . . .

CATHOLICS BELIEVE

1. Jesus is present in the Christian assembly, in the Word, and in the breaking of the bread.
2. The Eucharist prepares Christians for their mission of spreading the Gospel.

KNOW

For each word in Column A, choose the best description from Column B.

Column A	Column B
___ 1. Apostle	a. The work a person is sent to do
___ 2. Cleopas	b. An English scholar, teacher, and priest who wrote about mission
___ 3. mission	c. The gathered Christian community in which Jesus is present
___ 4. Mass	d. Part of the concluding rite of the Mass
___ 5. assembly	e. A follower of Jesus who met him on the road to Emmaus
___ 6. final blessing	f. A word that means "one who is sent"
___ 7. John Henry Newman	g. A name for the Eucharist that means sending forth

SUNDAY MASS

Carefully read several of the final blessing prayers used at Mass. Your teacher will help you find them. Then write your own prayer of blessing. At Mass, listen intently to hear which prayer the priest uses to complete the celebration.

Thanks and Praise!

Work together to plan and celebrate a class Mass. Form four committees: Readings, Prayers, Music, and Hospitality. Use the checklists and guidelines on these pages to help you plan.

◆ READINGS CHECKLIST
___ Choose readings

___ Choose lectors

___ Practice readings

◆ PRAYERS CHECKLIST
___ Write petitions

___ Choose readers for petitions

___ Choose a memorial acclamation

◆ MUSIC CHECKLIST
___ Get musician(s)

___ Choose songs

___ Practice songs

◆ HOSPITALITY CHECKLIST
___ Choose greeters

___ Choose servers

___ Choose gift bearers

◆ READINGS PLANNER
Choose one of these readings.

First Reading

___ Isaiah 12:3–5

___ Exodus 16:4–6

Responsorial Psalm

___ Psalm 105:1–4

___ Psalm 111:1–4

Second Reading

___ Philippians 1:3–7

___ 1 Corinthians 11:23–26

Gospel Reading

___ Luke 17:11–17

___ John 6:1–14

◆ MUSIC PLANNER

Opening song: _____ , page _____

Gospel Acclamation: _____

Presentation of the gifts: _____ , page _____

Communion song: _____ , page _____

Closing song: _____ , page _____

◆ PRAYER PLANNER

Prayer of the Faithful

Prayer for the leaders of the Church:

_____

Prayer for our country:

_____

Prayer for people in need:

_____

Prayer for the people of our parish:

_____

Prayer for our class:

_____

Memorial Acclamation:

_____

◆ HOSPITALITY PLANNER

Greeters: _____

Servers: _____

Gift bearers: _____

UNIT 3 REVIEW

LEARNING

1. How does the Church celebrate?
As a community, the Church celebrates holy times—feasts and seasons—in a holy place.

2. What is the Liturgy of the Word?
The Liturgy of the Word is the part of the Mass during which the Word of God in Scripture is proclaimed.

3. What is the Liturgy of the Eucharist?
The Liturgy of the Eucharist is the part of the Mass during which the sacrifice of Jesus is remembered and made present.

4. In what ways is Jesus present at Mass?
Jesus is present in the Christian assembly, in the Word, and in the Body and Blood of Christ.

5. What are Catholics sent out from Mass to do?
Catholics are sent out from Mass to carry out the mission of Jesus in the world.

ASKING

1. In what way do I understand the Eucharist better after studying this unit?
2. What can I do to celebrate the Eucharist better at Mass and with my family?

PRAYING

All:	Alleluia!
Group 1:	Praise the Lord in his sanctuary, praise him in the firmament of his strength.
Group 2:	Praise him for his mighty deeds, praise him for his sovereign majesty.
All:	Alleluia!
Group 1:	Praise him with the blast of trumpet, praise him with lyre and harp.
Group 2:	Praise him with timbrel and dance, praise him with strings and pipe.
All:	Alleluia!
Group 1:	Praise him with sounding cymbals, praise him with clanging cymbals.
Group 2:	Let everything that has breath praise the Lord!
All:	Alleluia!

PSALM 150

LIVING

You go to Mass on Sunday, but you are called to live the life of Jesus every day. Keep a log of how you practice these attitudes and actions every day this week.

Eucharist in Action	Say Thanks	Offer a Sacrifice	Remember God's Love	Share with Someone

The Church is a body composed of different members. It has a heart, a heart burning with love. Love, in fact, is the vocation which includes all others; it's a universe of its own, comprising all time and space—it's eternal!

Saint Thérèse of Lisieux

I Serve

Saint Clement's Parish Habitat for Humanity

LOVE ONE ANOTHER

As I have loved you, so you also should love one another.

JOHN 13:34

WHERE'S THE LOVE?

What loving action do you find in each of these stories? What do these actions accomplish? Write your answers in the spaces below.

THE SHOT

This was it. If Marissa made this shot, her team would win. She was nervous, but she had made plenty of penalty shots before. Her kick was straight and true—oh, no, it hit the post! Marissa felt sick all over. She had let the team down. Just then, all of her teammates arrived and gave her the biggest hug she had ever received. Marissa felt as if she had won the game.

A LITTLE HELP

Everyone else was already at recess, and Bart was rushing to catch up. On his way out of the classroom, he bumped into Andy's desk, sending books, papers, and pencils tumbling out. Hector, who often didn't get along well with Bart, helped Bart pick up the mess.

A STRIKE

Clay thought Gary's birthday bowling party was going to be great, except that Angela was on his team. Angela was such a good bowler. Clay could never be as good as she was. At the party, Angela showed Clay how to make a difficult spare. When Clay made a strike, Angela cheered.

Do As I Do

"**I** was the youngest of his Apostles, and often the quietest, too. But I always listened and watched carefully—not just to Jesus, but to the way people responded to him. That's the way it was that last night. He had a look that said he knew exactly what he was doing. He wanted to teach us one last thing. Looking back now, I believe it was the hardest thing we ever had to learn.

When we sat down at the table, I knew something was really different. We had never come to any Passover meal with dusty feet. Yet this time we did. We had been in the city all day making preparations for Passover. When the others began to arrive in the upper room, there was just no time to wash.

We were all taken by surprise by what Jesus did then. He stood up, took off his cloak, and wrapped a towel around his waist. Walking over to Philip, he poured water into a basin and started untying Philip's sandals.

This was not good. For Jesus to wash Philip's feet was unacceptable. A teacher would never be a servant to a student. Never! Philip put out his hand to stop Jesus. "What are you doing, Lord?" he asked "you know that washing a person's feet is such a lowly task that not even a slave may be forced to do it."

"No one forces me, Philip," whispered Jesus. "I choose to do this." Then he took Philip's feet and washed them, first his right foot and then his left.

Jesus the Servant

I had seen Jesus serve others before. He healed the sick. He fed the hungry. He was never afraid to get his hands dirty. But this was different. I can tell you, this was more than just about washing feet. It was so humbling. After all, we were watching our leader kneel before each of us to wash our feet.

When Jesus came to Peter's place, Peter objected loudly, "No, Master! You will never wash my feet."

"Unless you let me do this for you, Peter, you will not be with me in heaven," Jesus said quietly.

Then Peter said, "In that case, Master, don't just wash my feet. Wash my head and my hands, too!"

Jesus smiled, "Peter, you don't need a bath. You are clean." One by one, Jesus washed the feet of us all.

When he finished, Jesus said, "Do you realize what I have done for you?" he asked. "If I, the master and teacher, have washed your feet, you ought to wash one another's feet. I have given you a model to follow, so that as I have done for you, so you should also do. I give you a new commandment: love one another" *(John 13:12,15,34)*.

The Church remembers Jesus' call to service at the evening Mass on Holy Thursday. After the homily, the celebrant of the Mass washes the feet of some parishioners. In Rome, the pope himself reenacts Jesus' sign of service.

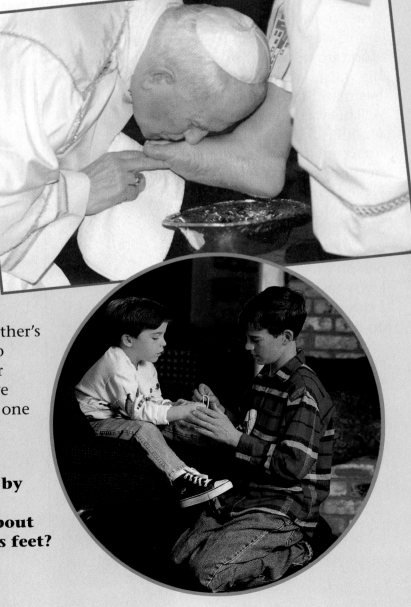

1. **What lesson was Jesus teaching his followers by washing their feet?**
2. **How would you feel about washing someone else's feet?**

FOLLOWING Jesus

Love was the reason Jesus served others and taught his followers to do the same. Jesus said, "No one has greater love than this, to lay down one's life for one's friends" *(John 15:13)*. You are probably not going to be called to die for Jesus. But you are called to follow Jesus' example of service. Choose one thing that you can do to give a little bit of your life to help others. Put your plan into action.

THE WORK OF LOVE

Jesus washed the feet of the Apostles because they were hot and dusty and needed to be washed. He wasn't afraid to roll up his sleeves, get down on his knees, and get messy.

The disciples understood the words Jesus used. Through his loving action, Jesus taught his friends, and you, how to show love for others. Those who minister must be as gentle as shepherds who care for frightened sheep. They must be as hardworking as field workers who quickly gather the grain when it is ripe.

The word *ministry* is used to describe this loving service to others. When you grow up, you may receive a call from God to serve in one of the Church's special ministries. Right now, your ministry is to show people love and respect.

HELP WANTED

Create a poster showing what it means to do Christian ministry. What work do ministers do? What rewards do ministers receive?

Love in Action

Read the stories of three Christians who showed people the love of God by their actions.

JEANNE JUGAN

When Jeanne was sixteen, she went to work as a kitchen maid for a rich woman. Together they visited the sick and the poor on the estate. Then Jeanne worked in a hospital, where she changed bandages and did a lot of the "dirty work" no one else wanted to do. She also shared the little money she earned with the poor.

People saw the work that Jeanne did and admired her for it. Several women joined Jeanne in her work. They formed a religious community called the Little Sisters of the Poor. Today, thousands of these sisters care for the poor, the homeless, and the elderly around the world.

DOMINIC SAVIO

Dominic grew up on the tough streets of a small town in Italy. Once two of his friends got so mad at each other that they planned to fight it out with rocks. Dominic tried to talk them out of it, but couldn't. So he made each of them agree to a secret condition which he would reveal just before the fight.

Dominic helped the boys pile up their rocks. Then he stood in the middle and announced his secret condition: they must each throw the first rock at him. There was no fight. Dominic Savio was named one of the youngest saints of the Church.

STAN CURTIS

Stan wondered what happened to the left over food from cafeteria steam tables. When he found out that this food was thrown away, Stan started a group called Kentucky Harvest. Volunteers take unwanted food from restaurants, hotels, hospitals, and grocery stores and deliver it to homeless shelters and soup kitchens. Sometimes they get day-old bread from the bakery. Once they received sixteen tons of mislabeled peanut butter, which the manufacturers could not sell and had planned to throw away. Today, a nationwide group called U.S.A. Harvest operates in many large cities.

ROLL UP YOUR SLEEVES

Like Jeanne, Dominic, and Stan, you can show love for others through your actions. Every Christian is called to the ministry of service through the sacrament of Baptism. To help you in your service to others, God has given you the gifts and strengths you need. Here are some things that you can do to be a better minister.

Be Yourself. *Use the gifts God has given you to help others. You will find your own wonderful ways to serve.*

Be Aware. *Look around for people who need your help, then reach out your hand to assist them.*

Be Concerned. *What do you think when you see a person standing on a street corner asking for change? In order to help this person, you must first learn to care for him or her. The secret is seeing Jesus in every person.*

Be Positive. *Jesus promised to be with you in this work. When it is hard to reach out or to offer help, remember that you do not work alone. Know that Jesus will help you achieve great things.*

1. **What do Jeanne Jugan, Dominic Savio, and Stan Curtis have in common?**
2. **What do the three stories teach you about loving others?**
3. **Share a story of your own. When has being a follower of Jesus made a difference in the way you acted?**

It's Up to You!

Jesus sees what people need today through your eyes. Jesus hears what people need through your ears. Jesus goes to people in need on your feet. Jesus helps people in their need through your hands. Tell one thing you could do in each of the following situations to make the situation better.

- You are ready to go swimming with your friends, but your towel is in the dryer. You notice that there is a load of clean, dry towels in the dryer.

  _____

- Your mom has asked you to go with her to visit your grandmother. Your friend wants you to go to a movie instead. Your mom says the choice is up to you.

  _____

- Two of your friends are angry at each other. They both ask you to be on their side.

  _____

Working for God

Father, you have called the ministers of your Church to follow the example of Jesus, who chose to serve others. May their work be your work. May they perform their ministry as Jesus did, with gentleness and concern for others.

Based on A PRAYER OF SAINT AUGUSTINE

WITH YOUR FAMILY

Your family doesn't put up a "Help Wanted" sign every time someone needs help. Or does it? Look for signs at home that tell you that someone needs your help. See how you can show your love by helping out at home.

CATHOLICS BELIEVE

1. Jesus gave his friends a new commandment of love.
2. All followers of Jesus are called to the ministry of service through the sacrament of Baptism.

KNOW

Choose **T** if the statement is true. Choose **F** if the statement is false.

T F 1. Jesus washed his friends' feet as a sign of how they should serve one another.

T F 2. The Church remembers Jesus' action of service on All Saints' Day.

T F 3. Jesus no longer serves people today.

T F 4. In Baptism, you receive gifts to help you carry out the ministry of service.

T F 5. Only priests and nuns are called to minister.

SUNDAY MASS

During Mass, people give money in the collection. This money is used to care for the needs of the Church and of the poor. Sometimes there are special collections for the work of a missionary. The next time you go to Mass, put some of your allowance in the collection. You may also contribute food to feed the hungry.

CONTENT KEYS

1. **The Holy Spirit bestows many gifts.**
2. **The community needs all the gifts of the Holy Spirit.**
3. **The gifts of the Holy Spirit are intended to be shared.**

> There are different forms of service but the same Lord.
> 1 CORINTHIANS 12:5

A TREASURE HUNT

Archaeologists on a dig don't know what they'll find. They could discover ancient pottery, the key to understanding a lost civilization, or maybe a great tomb. Or they could find nothing at all because they are looking in the wrong place.

Go on a treasure hunt within your self. What God-given gifts and talents do you have? On the chart, check off the gifts you know you have. Circle the ones you aren't sure about yet. Write in any gifts or talents you have that aren't on the list.

My Gifts and Talents

THAT'S ME	I'M GOOD AT	I'M INTERESTED IN
Caring	Dancing	Acting
Forgiving	Organizing	Astronomy
Adventurous	Leading	Religion
Friendly	Music	Skateboarding
Funny	Sports	Animals
Hopeful	Writing	Computer games

DREAM TEAM

"I don't get it!" Ricky said to his dad. "I'm really good at soccer. I can do just about anything. But the coach keeps holding me back. She makes me play the same boring position. She benched me just because I cut in front of Darla to score. 'Play your position!' That's all she ever says!"

"Is that so?" asked his dad. "The same thing happened to me when I was your age. I thought I could shoot better than anyone else on the team. And I also believed I should do most of the shooting. I wanted to be the star. But the coach didn't see it my way. He kept talking about teamwork. I can still hear that deep voice of his: 'Greg, soccer is a team sport. It's more important for the whole team to be good on fundamentals than for one player to be a star.' I heard what he said, but I didn't like it. Then I got injured and was out for ten games. I was shocked when the team kept winning without me.

"Ricky, teams where everyone works together win a lot more games than those that have a lot of individual stars. Use your gifts, boy, but use them for the benefit of the team. Play your position, not everyone else's. Even a star is only a part of the team."

"Yeah, dad, I hear you, but I don't like it," said Ricky as he headed for bed.

NIGHT GAME

That night Ricky had a dream. He was dribbling toward the goal. Two opponents closed in on him fast. Ricky tried to pass the ball, but it was snatched away. His teammate Emma had taken the ball. Now she was trying to shoot.

What's Emma doing out here? She's supposed to be playing defense, thought Ricky. Suddenly Ricky was surrounded by all of his teammates. What are they doing, thought Ricky. We'll never score if we all play like that. This is crazy!

Ricky watched in disbelief. As Emma started to shoot, one of her own teammates came up from behind, stole the ball, and took the shot.

That's when Ricky woke up, breathing heavily. "What an awful dream!" he said. "Now I get it. Work as a team! Play your position!" Smiling, he drifted back to sleep.

ONE BODY

Read 1 Corinthians 12:12–27. Using Saint Paul's thoughts, write your own statement about what it means to work together as a team.

1. **What lesson did Ricky learn in his dream?**
2. **What are some gifts that players on a team need?**
3. **What are some gifts that help people work together as a team?**

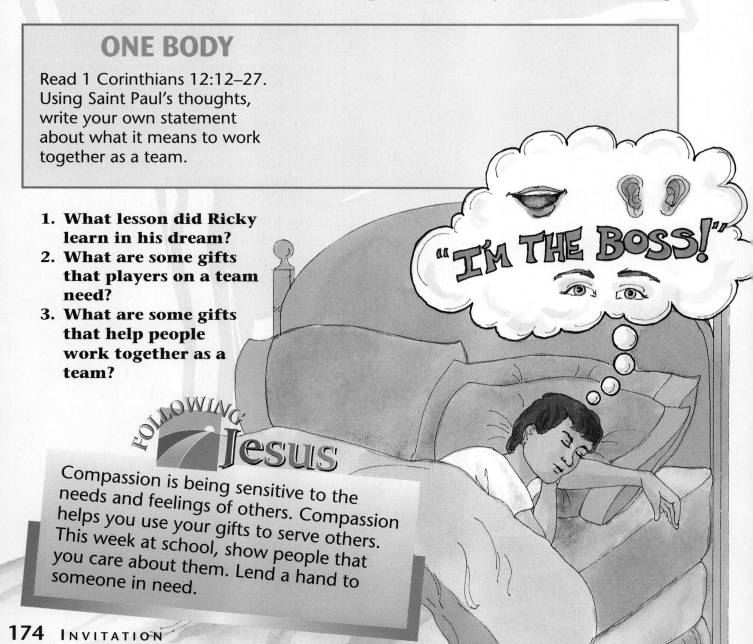

FOLLOWING Jesus

Compassion is being sensitive to the needs and feelings of others. Compassion helps you use your gifts to serve others. This week at school, show people that you care about them. Lend a hand to someone in need.

The Parable of the Gold Coins

A rich man was going to a country far away. Before he left, he called his servants and gave each of them a gold coin. "See what you can do with this while I am gone," he told them.

After a long time, the master returned and called his servants to report to him. The first one said, "Sir, I have earned ten gold coins with the one you gave me."

"Well done! You are a good servant," the master commended him. "Come and share my joy."

The second servant then reported, "Sir, I have earned five gold coins with the one you gave me." To this one the master said also, "You are a good servant. Come and share my joy."

Finally, the last servant came before the master. Here is my gold coin," he said, "I have kept it safely hidden in my handkerchief." The master was sad and angry.

"Take the coin away from him and give it to the one who has ten," he ordered. "Then throw this worthless fellow out of my house!"

Based on MATTHEW 25:14–30 *and* LUKE 19:11–27

Gift Exchange

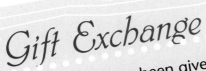

You may not have been given any gold coins lately, but God has given you an abundance of gifts and talents.

Tell about a time when you used one of your gifts to serve another person. Tell about a time when someone used his or her gifts to help you.

Someone Helped Me	Gift Used
I Helped Someone	Gift Used

TRUTH IN PARABLES

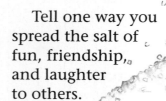

Jesus told many parables explaining the need for Christians to serve others. Here are a few examples.

SALT

"You are the salt of the earth," said Jesus *(Matthew 5:13)*. If you have ever eaten soup that was made with no salt, you know how flat and flavorless it is. A little salt is needed to bring the rest of the ingredients to life. Like some of those hidden treasures you found in yourself, salt is not visible in the soup. But what a difference it makes!

Tell one way you spread the salt of fun, friendship, and laughter to others.

_____

_____

_____

LIGHT

"You are the light of the world," said Jesus. "A city set on a mountain cannot be hidden. Nor does a person light a lamp and then put it under a bushel basket; it is set on a lampstand, where it gives light to all in the house. Just so, your light must shine before others, that they may see your good deeds and glorify your heavenly Father" *(Matthew 5:14–16)*.

Tell one way you bring the light of understanding or compassion to others.

_____

_____

_____

If you have ever been scared of the dark or tried to find your path through a dark wood, you know how comforting and helpful light can be. By calling his disciples to be light, Jesus asked them to go into the dark corners of the world and eliminate the darkness. He asked them to be a guiding light that leads others to God. What was Jesus asking of you when he called his followers to be light?

At Your Service

Every baptized person is called to ministry. When you follow Jesus by how you act, work, and play, you are involved in ministry. Bishops, priests, and deacons are ordained for particular roles in the Church. The rest of the baptized—married men and women, members of religious communities, and even you—participate in lay ministry.

In the sacrament of Baptism, every follower of Jesus receives the gifts and strengths necessary for a special ministry of service. "As each one has received a gift, use it to serve one another as stewards of God's varied grace" *(1 Peter 4:10)*.

A Light in the Darkness

When Germany invaded France in 1940, Blessed Marcel Callo was twenty-one years old. He and other young French workers were deported to Germany and put to work making weapons. They were treated like prisoners, forced to work long hours, and given bad food.

Instead of complaining, Marcel found ways to lift the spirits of his fellow workers. He tried to make sure that everyone got enough to eat, organized games, and put on plays to entertain the men. He gathered the workers for Bible study and prayers.

Marcel's actions came to the attention of the Nazis. They sent him to a prison camp for being a Catholic. Beaten and starved, Marcel died in prison just two months before the war ended.

1. **Explain in your own words the meaning of the parable of the gold coins.**
2. **Give an example of lay ministry.**
3. **What treasures did Marcel Callo share with his fellow workers?**

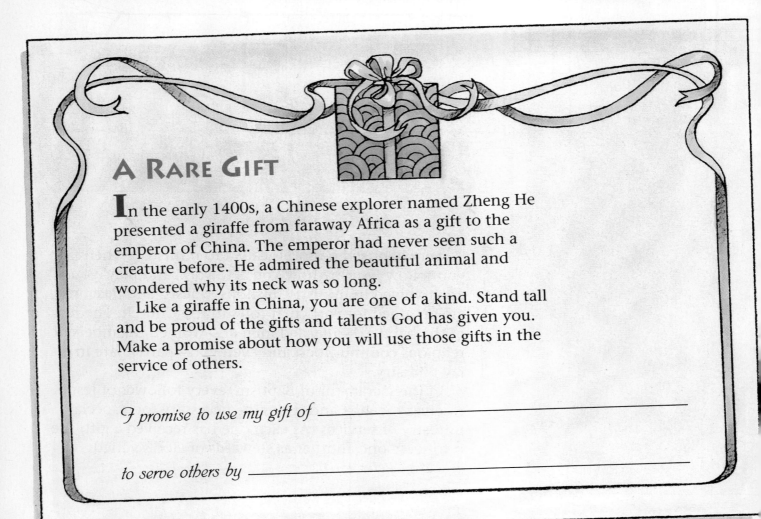

A Rare Gift

In the early 1400s, a Chinese explorer named Zheng He presented a giraffe from faraway Africa as a gift to the emperor of China. The emperor had never seen such a creature before. He admired the beautiful animal and wondered why its neck was so long.

Like a giraffe in China, you are one of a kind. Stand tall and be proud of the gifts and talents God has given you. Make a promise about how you will use those gifts in the service of others.

I promise to use my gift of _____

to serve others by _____

A Source of Light

God our Father, let us bring the light of your son, Jesus, to everyone. Allow us to warm the world with your love. Strengthen us by your Holy Spirit to use our gifts to serve wherever we are needed. Let us one day join our tiny lights with the eternal light of your heavenly kingdom. Amen.

WITH YOUR FAMILY

This week, take a new look at your family. What gifts and talents does each member of your family have? People will use their gifts more freely if you encourage them. Thank your mom, dad, or grandparent for listening, cooking, or telling you a joke. Let your brother and sister know that you admire something they do.

CATHOLICS BELIEVE

1. There are many gifts, but one Spirit working in all.
2. Jesus calls Christians to use their gifts to serve others.

KNOW

Complete each sentence by filling in the missing word or words.

1. Jesus said that his followers were to be the _____ of the earth and the _____ of the world.
2. The ministry practiced by all of the baptized is called _____ ministry.
3. The master rewarded the good servant by saying this to him: "_____ _____ _____ _____ _____."
4. Saint Paul reminded the Corinthians that followers of Jesus are all members of one _____
5. Lay ministry is the way you use your gifts to _____ _____ in everyday life.

SUNDAY MASS

There are many ways that you can serve the parish community at Mass. You can bring up the gifts. You can serve as a greeter, a lector, an usher, or a musician. Use your gifts for the benefit of others. Get involved!

TAKE THIS RING

CONTENT KEYS

1. **Marriage is a covenant relationship.**
2. **Jesus is present in the love of the married couple.**
3. **Marriage is a sacrament of service.**

My love shall never leave you.

ISAIAH 54:10

A MARRIAGE MADE IN HEAVEN

Tobiah and his companion (the angel Raphael in disguise) were looking for a woman for Tobiah to marry. Raphael said, "Tonight we must stay with Raguel. He has a daughter, an only child, named Sarah. She is very beautiful, courageous, and sensible, and her family loves her dearly. Ask her father to let you have Sarah as your bride."

But Tobiah protested, "I have heard about Sarah, and I am afraid to marry her. They say she has been married seven times already and that each of her husbands died on his wedding night."

"Trust me, Tobiah," said Raphael. "You have nothing to fear. Sarah was destined for you by God before the world existed. She will be a good wife, and you will be blessed with children. You have no need to worry."

Tobiah trusted God and fell deeply in love with Sarah. On the night of their wedding, Tobiah and Sarah prayed, "God of heaven and all creation, pour down your blessings on our love and our life together. Let us live together to a happy old age. Amen, amen." God did bless their marriage, which was long and prosperous.

Based on TOBIT 4–10

1. **In what ways does this Bible story describe marriage as a gift of God?**
2. **Based upon this story, what would you say are the benefits of marriage?**

LOVE, MARRIAGE, AND LACE CURTAINS

"Happy anniversary, honey," crooned Dwight, sneaking up behind Karen and giving her a big hug.

"It's not till tomorrow, Dwight," she laughed.

"I know, I just can't wait any longer. Here, open your present," said Dwight, shoving a big box into her arms.

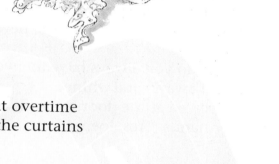

Cautiously, Karen opened the box, then gasped, "Lace curtains. Just like at our honeymoon cottage!" Karen danced around their small living room with the lace curtains, tears sparkling in her eyes.

Then she stopped. "We can't afford these."

"Why do you think I've been working all that overtime lately?" Dwight teased. "Come on, let's put up the curtains in our bedroom."

LOVE, CHILDREN, AND BLUE CUPS

"Mommy," two-year-old Joey's sleepy voice called from the next room. Dwight opened one eye and looked over at Karen, who was sound asleep. Then he glanced at the alarm clock beside the bed: 2 A.M. He groaned.

"I'm coming, son," Dwight answered softly through the darkness.

"I want Mommy," demanded Joey when Dwight arrived. Dwight smiled. "Let's let Mommy sleep, sport. She'll come next time."

Joey said, "Okay, Daddy. I want a drink of water."

"Coming right up," Dwight promised. When he returned, Joey took the cup and said, "I love you, Daddy."

"I love you, too, Joey. Sleep tight, now."

LOVE, FRIENDSHIP, AND LASAGNA

Joe banged the screen door and bounded into the kitchen. "Has anyone seen my glove?" he asked.

He stopped in his tracks. "Mom, something smells great!" Then he spotted the big pan of lasagna cooling on the kitchen counter.

Karen called from the laundry room. "Don't get into that lasagna, Joe. It's for the Daltons. Mrs. Dalton came home from the hospital yesterday with the new baby."

"Aw, Mom, do you always have to give the good stuff away?" Joe whined.

Karen appeared at the doorway with a towel in her hands. "Yes, Joe, we're supposed to give the good stuff away— good stuff like friendship, love, and lasagna. But that just makes more for us to share. If you hadn't noticed, there's another pan of lasagna in the oven."

Karen couldn't help but laugh at the look of relief on Joe's face.

LOVE, FAMILY, AND GRAY HAIR

"To my wonderful parents," announced Karen as she raised a glass of wine for a toast. She gazed down the long table at the gray-haired man and woman. "You have been an inspiration to me and Dwight. I pray that we will be blessed, as you have been, with forty wonderful years together."

Karen's father stood up to acknowledge the toast. "Wonderful, yes. The ride of a lifetime," he mused.

He smiled at his family and friends assembled to celebrate. "We couldn't have made it without all of you—and the grace of God. Thank you, one and all."

Partners for Life

Become an investigative reporter. Talk to a married couple. Ask them to describe some of the ways their marriage has changed over the years. From what you learn from the couple, write a newspaper story about married life.

WEDDING RINGS

A quilt is a bed cover made from small scraps of colorful cloth that are pieced into a pattern and then sewn together carefully by hand. One of the most beautiful quilt patterns is called the wedding ring.

When a man and woman marry, they exchange rings, saying to each other, "Take this ring as a sign of my love and fidelity. In the name of the Father, and of the Son, and of the Holy Spirit."

Fidelity means faithfulness. The exchange of rings is a sign of lasting love. A husband and wife promise to be true to each other in good times and in bad times, for all of their lives. This is a very important promise. That is why a couple should be sure of their love before they marry.

Making a marriage work is a lot like making a quilt. It takes time and careful work to make a marriage. One person can't do it alone. Over time, a husband and wife cut and piece, patch and sew, fix mistakes, and mend the rips and tears of their life together. They create special memories and experiences to fit into their own unique pattern.

A marriage is a work of art in progress. As the marriage partners grow and change, the grace of the sacrament continues to help them. The marriage isn't finished until one of the partners dies.

Circles of Love

Inside the rings, write some important pieces of your family's life together. For example, you could write the names of your parents and the date of their wedding, or the names and birth dates of each child in your family.

THE SACRAMENT OF MARRIAGE

In the sacrament of Marriage, a man and a woman bind themselves together forever. This is God's plan, and this is what every newly married couple wants. The words and the gestures used in the celebration of Marriage are signs that God is present in the union of the man and woman.

The promises, or marriage vows, a couple shares with each other are the key words of the sacrament of Marriage. Before God, a man and a woman promise to love one another faithfully as long as they both live. They promise to share their love with others, accepting children lovingly from God. They promise to help one another on their journey together through life. Because the bride and groom make these promises to each other, they (not the priest) are the ministers of the sacrament.

The Church blesses the promises the husband and wife make to each other. The priest or deacon and the community of family and friends gathered for the wedding act as witnesses. The whole Church promises to support the couple, to pray for them, and to be with them in difficult times.

The promises of marriage show that a covenant exists between the couple and God. The Church shares in the covenant agreement by promising to support the married couple.

WEDDING BELLS

Marriage is a sacrament, a sign of God's faithful love. The sacrament is usually celebrated during Mass. The priest or the deacon asks the man and woman if they have freely chosen to marry and to be faithful to one another. The priest or deacon also asks if they will accept children and raise them as members of the Church. The bride and groom answer yes to each question. By joining their lives in this way, the couple becomes a sign of God's love in the world. By becoming a family, they are a sign of new life.

AFTER THE CAKE

Marriage is a vocation, a call from God to serve others and to share God's love with others. Marriage, single life, priesthood, and religious life are all vocations. In Marriage, a man and woman give themselves to each other, just as Jesus gave himself for all people. In their daily lives, in both big and little ways, a married couple serve one another with love. Together they share their love with their children, their families, their friends, and those in need.

1. **What is meant by the words *marriage covenant*?**
2. **In what ways is the couple a sign of God's love?**
3. **What is the meaning of the wedding rings?**

STRINGS ATTACHED

What are some of the ways parents share the gift of love with their children?

FOLLOWING Jesus

Jesus was a good friend. He was there when his friends needed him. A husband and a wife must also learn to be good friends if they want their marriage to be happy.

You can learn how to be a good friend. Practice listening to what others have to say. Show appreciation for gifts. Try to be kind. Be prepared to stand by your friend when he or she is in trouble. Learn to enjoy what your friend likes. Don't always expect things to go your way.

THE FAMILY CIRCLE

Marriage is often called the sacrament of family, or the domestic church. It is in the family that you first learn how to follow Jesus' example of loving service.

Think of ways you can serve others in your family. Fill in each part of the circle by telling how each person or persons serves others. Share your answers with your classmates and your family.

FAMILIES • YOU • HUSBAND AND WIFE • PARENTS • CHILDREN • BROTHERS AND SISTERS •

A PRAYER OF BLESSING

Ask God to help your family follow Jesus' example of loving service.

Holy Father, creator of the universe, you have made us for love. Let us rejoice always in your blessings and gifts of love.

Grant all married men and women a long life in the company of their friends, until you call them at last to rest in your eternal life.

Amen.

WITH YOUR FAMILY

Do you ever stop and think about all of the great things your family does for you? During the next week, write down on a piece of paper every kind action and every benefit you receive from your family. Try to say thank you to the people in your family who do these things for you.

CATHOLICS BELIEVE

1. The sacrament of Marriage celebrates a covenant between a man and a woman.
2. In the sacrament of Marriage, a couple promises to be faithful to each other, to accept children lovingly from God, and to serve others.

KNOW

Complete each sentence by choosing the right word from within the parentheses.

1. The Church celebrates Marriage as a (sacrament, custom).
2. The vows, or promises, of Marriage are a sign of the (bargain, covenant) between the husband and wife.
3. Christian marriage is intended to be a (temporary, lifelong) commitment.
4. As part of the wedding ceremony, the couple exchanges (rings, candles) as a sign of their love and fidelity.
5. Fidelity means (obedience, faithfulness).
6. The minister of the sacrament of Marriage is the (couple, priest).

SUNDAY MASS

Saint Paul wrote that the relationship between Jesus and the Church is like the relationship between a husband and a wife. Jesus is the bridegroom, and his bride is the Church. This statement means that Jesus loves and is faithful to the Church. Because you are part of the Church, Jesus makes this same promise to you. At Mass this week, renew your covenant relationship with Jesus by meaning the words you pray.

FEED MY LAMBS

CONTENT KEYS

1. **Holy Orders celebrates ordained ministry.**
2. **Bishops, priests, and deacons are ordained.**
3. **Holy Orders is a sacrament of service.**

Tend the flock of God in your midst, willingly, as God would have it.

1 PETER 5:2

MEET BISHOP O'BRIEN

We were finishing up our last Confirmation class, when we met our new bishop. I didn't think he looked anything like a bishop. He was dressed in black, like a priest, but he also wore a Minnesota Twins cap.

"Good morning," Bishop O'Brien said with a smile. "I'll be here at the parish all weekend, for your confirmation and the Sunday Masses. Any Twins fans here?"

MEET FATHER MEL

Our new pastor, Father Mel, is a down-to-earth sort of guy. He never acts phony, whether he's talking to you in the parking lot or giving the homily at Mass. He's so cool that when the collection basket is passed, he always puts money in the basket.

MEET DEACON HALL

John Hall builds recreational vehicles. He is also the deacon at our parish. Deacon Hall is married and has five children. His daughter Martha and I are in scouts together.

Deacon Hall gives the homily at Mass about once a month. Each Sunday evening he meets with a group of people from the parish who are out of work. They talk, pray, and share news about getting a job.

THE GOOD SHEPHERD

"**J**esus, if you wish, you can make me clean," pleaded the leper *(Mark 1:40).*

"My daughter is dying. Please lay your hands on her that she may get well and live," begged Jairus *(Mark 5:23).*

"Son of David, have pity on us," the blind men said *(Matthew 9:27).*

Like waves rolling onto the shore, crowds of people came to Jesus. All of these people had their own pain, their own trouble. Jesus was aware of each person's need, and it moved his heart deeply. "Sheep without a shepherd could not be more troubled or abandoned," he said.

That night, Jesus did not sleep at all. He spent the hours in prayer, asking God to bless those he had chosen to be his shepherds. The next day, he sent his disciples to heal people of their illnesses, raise the dead, cleanse lepers, drive out demons, forgive sins, and baptize people—all in his name.

As for his newly chosen shepherds, Jesus told them not to buy fancy clothes or stay in expensive hotels. They were to take nothing with them. They were to depend on God for everything. They were to be concerned about the needs of the people, not their own.

CALLING NEW SHEPHERDS

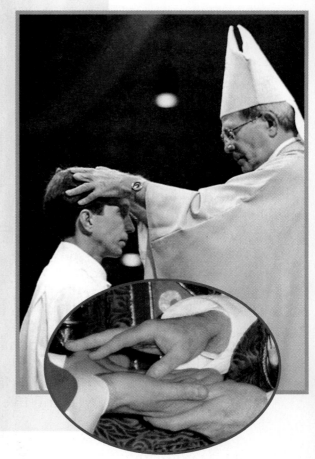

Imagine that you are one of the Twelve Apostles. Most of the Twelve, including you, have traveled to far-off countries to spread the Gospel.

You have been very successful in spreading the Good News. In just a short time, the number of believers has grown so rapidly that you cannot take care of them all. You realize that you need to have other people to help you do the Lord's work. What kind of people will you choose? What work will you have them do?

Fortunately for you, some of the other Apostles have already faced this same problem. They have left you written suggestions to help you answer your questions. Find each of the Scripture passages listed below, read them, and answer the questions that follow. Then describe the qualities of the people you will choose to help you. Explain the type of work each person will do.

Titus 1:7–9

What five qualities should a bishop have?

What should a bishop believe?

Acts 20:17,28

What is the ministry of the leader?

1 Peter 5:1–3

How should priests care for God's flock?

James 5:14–15

What can the priest do for a person who is sick?

Acts 6:1–4

What is the job of the deacon?

1 Timothy 3:8–9

How should a deacon act?

How will your helpers act? What work will they do?

A Bishop and a Deacon

In the year 258, the Roman emperor Valerian ordered the Christians to stop believing in Jesus and to worship the Roman gods. The penalty for any Christian who refused to offer sacrifice to the pagan gods would be death.

The Christians in Rome chose to disobey the Emperor's command. They continued to meet secretly, celebrating the Lord's Supper in the catacombs, the underground cemeteries of Rome. Pope Sixtus, the bishop of Rome, celebrated the Eucharist with them. On August 6 of that year, Roman soldiers broke into the house where Sixtus was teaching the people about Jesus. They arrested Sixtus and four deacons who were with him.

When deacon Lawrence heard what had happened, he hurried to the house where Sixtus was being held under guard. "I should have been with you," protested Lawrence.

"I am not going without you, my son," said Sixtus. "In three days time you will be joining me. In the meantime, take all of the money that belongs to the Church and give it to the poor. Sell the sacred vessels and give that money also to the poor. Go quickly now, and take care of this."

The guards overheard this conversation and reported it to an officer. Thinking that the Christians had a lot of money, the officer ordered Lawrence to turn over the treasure of the Church to Valerian which Lawrence promised to do in three days.

On the third day, after giving the Church's money to the poor, Lawrence presented a crowd of people to the Roman official. "These are the treasures of the Church," Lawrence declared. The faithful deacon was put to death three days after the courageous bishop.

Following Jesus

Every day Jesus calls you to serve others in small ways. "Come," Jesus may say to you, "Help Mrs. Redding carry her groceries up the stairs." "Come, clean out the guinea pig's cage as you told your mom you would." "Come, take your little sister out to play." Tonight, think about how Jesus called you to serve others today. Think about how you responded. Do this every night this week. Ask Jesus to help you to follow him.

THE SACRAMENT OF HOLY ORDERS

Jesus called twelve of his followers to accept the duties of apostle. Jesus continues to call some people out of all the baptized Christians to ordained ministry. The word *ordained* means "appointed," or "set in order." Ordained ministers receive the sacrament of Holy Orders, which gives them the responsibility and grace to serve God's people.

CELEBRATING HOLY ORDERS

The ordination of a bishop, priest, or deacon includes the sign of laying on of hands. This gesture calls on the Holy Spirit to fill the newly ordained person with strength and grace.

Anointing with oil is also part of the celebration. A bishop's head is anointed as a sign of leadership. A priest's hands are anointed as a sign of his ministry to offer the sacrifice of the Mass.

THE ORDER OF BISHOP

Bishops are ordained to teach, to lead, and to serve the whole Church. It is their duty to teach the Gospel, to lead the people in being faithful to the Church, and to serve as a shepherd of the People of God.

Bishops are successors of the Apostles. Their ministry has been handed down from bishop to bishop from the time of Jesus. An individual bishop has responsibility for a particular diocese, or group of Catholic parishes.

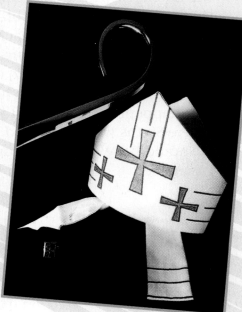

The bishop wears or carries three signs of his office.

1. A ring, as a sign of his fidelity to the Church.
2. A miter, the tall hat that a bishop wears in processions.
3. A crosier, a staff shaped like a shepherd's crook. A bishop is the pastor, or shepherd, of the diocese.

THE ORDER OF PRIEST

Priests are ordained to preach the Word of God and to celebrate the sacraments. They work closely with the bishop. In the early Church, priests were called presbyters or elders. They helped the bishops by preaching and presiding at the celebration of the Eucharist.

At ordination, the priest is given a chalice and paten, the vessels used for the Eucharist, as a sign of the ministry of celebrating the sacrament. He is given the stole and chasuble, the liturgical vestments of the priest. Priests wear their stoles draped around their necks with the ends hanging freely.

DID YOU KNOW?

The pope—the successor of Saint Peter and the chief teacher and shepherd of God's People—is the bishop of Rome. He is chosen from among all of the bishops to lead the Church. The title pope comes from the Latin word for father. One title for the pope is the Servant of the Servants of God.

THE ORDER OF DEACON

Deacons are ordained to serve the community. Sometimes the deacon's service is liturgical, as in preaching a homily or celebrating Baptism. Sometimes the service of the deacon is charitable, as in visiting the sick or caring for the needs of the poor. Deacons are chosen to serve the needs of the community. They assist the bishop and priests in the diocese in which they serve.

At ordination, the deacon is given a Book of the Gospels—a sign of the ministry of preaching the Word—and a stole, the liturgical vestment of a deacon. A deacon wears the stole looped across the left shoulder and joined at the right hip.

1. What are the three orders of ordained ministry in the Church?
2. Explain the sign of laying on of hands used in Holy Orders.
3. How were Pope Saint Sixtus and Saint Lawrence faithful to their ministry?

TREASURES OF THE CHURCH

The Church has many treasures, as Saint Lawrence showed. Your diocese and parish have many treasures as well. On the jewels, write the names of the bishop(s) of your diocese, your pastor and other parish priests, and the deacon(s) who serve your parish or diocese. Then write the names of some of the other people who serve in your parish, such as your teacher and the parish secretary. Be sure to put your own name in one of the jewels.

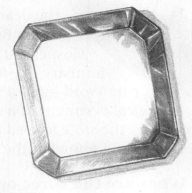

WITH YOUR FAMILY

Placing your hands upon another person's head is a sign of blessing. This week, try an experiment. Express your love for other members of your family through touch: give a bear hug, stroke an arm, place a hand on a shoulder, pat someone on the hand, or give someone a neck rub. What response do you get back from this loving gesture?

WE PRAISE YOU

The *Te Deum* is a song of rejoicing that was written in the early fifth century. The song is sung at the consecration of a bishop. Pray these words as a prayer of thanksgiving for ministers who serve the Church.

You are God: We praise you!
You are the Lord: We praise you!
You are the eternal Creator:
All creation worships you!
Father of majesty, your only Son, and the
Holy Spirit, our guide.
You are Christ, and you opened the kingdom of
heaven to all believers.
Come then, Lord, and help your people,
and bring us with your saints
to glory everlasting.

CATHOLICS BELIEVE

1. The sacrament of Holy Orders celebrates the call to serve God's People through the ordained ministry.
2. Ordained ministers of the Church are bishops, priests, and deacons.

KNOW

Fill in the missing word on each line.

1. The laying on of _____ is a sign of ordination.
2. The "Servant of the Servants of God" is the _____ .
3. Priests and bishops are _____ with _____ at ordination.
4. Bishops are successors of the _____ .
5. Holy Orders is a sacrament of _____ .
6. The _____ is ordained to preach the Gospel and to assist the bishop and the priest in serving the community.
7. The _____ is ordained to share the word and to celebrate the sacraments.
8. The _____ is ordained to teach and serve as the leader of a diocese.

SUNDAY MASS

In the Eucharistic Prayer of the Mass, the priest prays for the pope and the bishops of your diocese, naming them personally in the prayer. This week when you go to Mass, listen for this part of the prayer and join your prayer with that of the priest.

WORK AND PRAY

CONTENT KEYS

1. Religious life is a vocation.
2. Religious communities are dedicated to prayer and service.
3. Poverty, chastity, and obedience are religious vows.

The community of believers was of one heart and mind, and no one claimed that any possession was his or her own, but they held everything in common.
FROM ACTS 4:32

QUEST FOR GOLD

The race lasted less than a minute. The winner was decided by less than .01 seconds. After years of work, dedication, sacrifice, and struggle, the gold medal is finally yours!

Winning an Olympic medal, or even qualifying to compete in the Olympic Games, is an amazing feat. Top athletes dedicate themselves entirely to their sport. They are driven by a vision to be the best.

People who are dedicated to a vision willingly make sacrifices in order to make their vision become a reality: hours of practice, few friends, little TV, special diets. Some young athletes even live apart from their families so they can be close to their trainers and training facilities. Whether or not they ever win a medal, they know that they have done all that they can to succeed.

GOING FOR THE GOLD

You may not ever win an Olympic medal, but you can accomplish your goals with planning & hard work. Decide one thing you'd like to achieve. Prepare a weekly schedule that you can follow that will help you reach your goal.

SUNDAY	MONDAY	TUESDAY	WEDNESDAY	THURSDAY	FRIDAY	SATURDAY

QUEST FOR GOD

Just as some people dedicate their lives to winning a gold medal, other people dedicate their lives to God. Saint Benedict was willing to make just that type of commitment to God.

Rome was the capital of the empire. Every sin, every evil, every vice ever invented could be found in Rome. But Rome was also the best place for a young boy to come if he wanted to know more about Jesus. And so twelve-year-old Benedict came to Rome.

Benedict lived with the lawlessness and sinfulness of Rome long enough to complete his education. Then he moved to the mountains outside of Rome. In the mountains, he was befriended by the hermit Romanus, who gave him a robe of animal skins and showed him a cave where he could live.

Benedict was so dedicated to God that he lived alone in the cave for three years, spending each waking moment in prayer. Each day, Romanus brought a portion of his own food for Benedict to eat. The cave was so hard to reach that Romanus had to lower the food down to Benedict in a basket.

Although Benedict never left his cave, word about him spread. People walked miles to seek his guidance and to ask for his blessing. Reports of miracles and healings soon followed.

RULES TO LIVE BY

Seeing Benedict's holiness, a small group of men came to join Benedict in prayer. They wanted to live like Benedict and to learn from him. To assist these young men on their path to God, Benedict created a set of religious rules for the men to follow:

- Pray constantly.
- Lovingly follow God's commandments.
- Fast until noon.
- Stop eating meat.
- Treat all people equally as brothers and sisters.

Benedict taught that work was a gift from God. He insisted that all of his followers do manual labor every day. "It is not shameful to work," he said. "Work is not only honorable, it can also lead to holiness."

"Pray and work" became one of the mottoes of Benedict's order. The monks lived according to Benedict's Rule. They were driven by Benedict's desire to follow Jesus in all things. This vision helped them continue when they were cold and hungry, lonely and tired.

1. **What is the Rule of Saint Benedict?**
2. **What about Benedict's way of life attracted people to his religious order?**

MY RULE OF LIFE

The Rule of Saint Benedict contains many practical lessons for living the Gospel—good advice for all followers of Jesus. Saint Benedict gave these mottoes:

- ▶ Honor all people.
- ▶ Do not seek soft living.
- ▶ Speak the truth from your heart and your mouth.
- ▶ Do not be a grumbler.
- ▶ Make peace with your enemies before sundown.

Write two rules that can help you follow Jesus in your own life.

_____

_____

_____

_____

_____

_____

Obedience is one of the ways that you are called to follow Jesus right now. This week, try to obey your parents, teachers, and other adults in charge immediately, without grumbling or complaining. Offer this act of sacrifice to Jesus as a prayer.

A Way of Life

The followers of Saint Benedict are known as Benedictines. They carried his way of life across Europe. Monasteries of religious men, called monks or brothers, and convents of religious women, called nuns, were founded in many towns and villages. Men and women joined these monasteries and convents in large numbers, attracted by the dedication, prayer, and life of the monks and nuns. For a time in the Middle Ages, the Rule of Saint Benedict was followed by every religious community in the Western world.

Religious communities, or religious orders, are groups of men or women who dedicate their lives to God and the service of the Church. They may be priests, brothers or sisters. The word *religious* means "bound to the Rule." Members of a religious community usually live together, support one another, and share their lives and work.

A Life of Love

Members of religious communities take Jesus' call to "come, follow me" very seriously. Religious men and women vow to live lives guided by the virtues of poverty, chastity, and obedience. These vows are rooted in the Gospel.

- **Poverty:** They promise to live a simple life, without being concerned about material possessions.

- **Chastity:** They promise to love Jesus and God's people, choosing service to the Church instead of marriage and family life.

- **Obedience:** They promise to obey God and the Rule of the community.

The Rich Young Man

Read the story of Jesus and the rich young man (*Matthew 19:16–30*). Tell how the story applies to the call to religious life.

THE WORK OF PRAYER

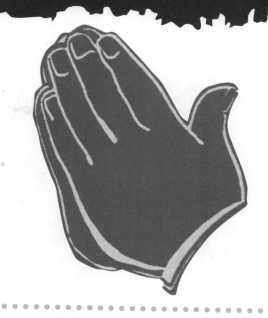

Prayer is one of the most important parts of religious life. Religious men and women have tried to follow Saint Paul's advice to "pray without ceasing" *(1 Thessalonians 5:17)*. In order to do this, Saint Benedict divided up the day and night into regular times of prayer.

They prayed by chanting the psalms and reading Scripture. This form of prayer is called the Liturgy of the Hours, which means "the work of prayer."

THE WORK OF SERVICE

Service is another important element of religious life. Over the centuries, religious men and women have served the Church and the world in many different ways. Each religious community tends to follow the charism, or special gift for ministry, of its founder. Some live in silent prayer, some are teachers, and some are lawyers, doctors or cooks. All are following Jesus' call in their own way.

MISSIONARY WORK
Some religious communities have dedicated their lives to spreading the Gospel message about Jesus to people of other lands as missionaries. Franciscan and Jesuit priests were among the first to bring the Gospel to North America. Today, members of American religious orders, such as the Maryknoll Missionaries, share the Good News around the world.

EDUCATION
During the early Middle Ages in Europe, monks and nuns kept art, literature, music, and learning alive. Many of the finest colleges and universities in the world were built or run by religious orders including the Jesuits, Dominicans, and Christian Brothers. The first schools for Catholic children in the United States were started by the Ursuline Sisters and by Mother Seton's Sisters of Charity.

HEALTH CARE
Early in the Christian era, hospitals were established as shelters run by monks for travelers who were ill or wounded, and for the poor, the blind, and the crippled. During the Civil War, Holy Cross Sisters served as battlefield nurses.

1. **Great athletes, musicians, dancers, and research scientists devote their entire lives to their sport, art, or work. In what ways are religious men and women like them?**
2. **What three vows do religious men and women make?**
3. **In what ways do these vows help a religious man or woman live a life of service?**

At the dinner table this evening, work with your family to develop a family motto. This motto will describe what your family thinks is important. It will be a brief summary of your family's vision. When you have developed the motto, write it on a clean piece of paper and hang it on the refrigerator for all to see.

YOUR CALL

Jesus said, "You shall love the Lord your God with all your heart, with all your soul, with all your mind, and with all your strength. And you shall love your neighbor as yourself" *(Mark 12:30–31).* This new commandment describes how a Christian is to live.

In the first space, write two or three ways you would like to serve God's people. In the second space, write a prayer for guidance, so that you may know what God is calling you to be.

WAYS I WOULD LIKE TO SERVE	PRAYER FOR MY VOCATION

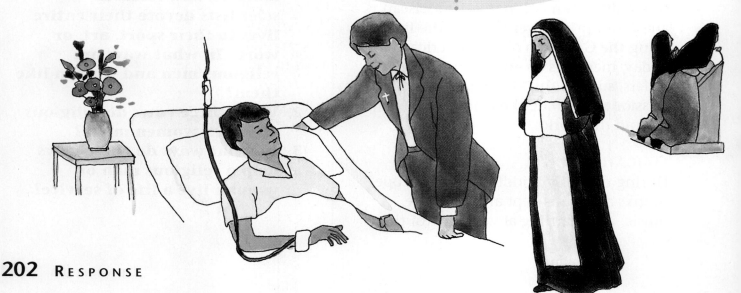

▼ REVIEW CHAPTER 23

CATHOLICS BELIEVE

1. Members of religious communities answer Jesus' call to follow him by dedicating their lives to prayer and service.
2. Members of religious communities make vows of poverty, chastity, and obedience.

KNOW

For each term in Column A, choose the best description from Column B.

Column A

_____ 1. Pray and work
_____ 2. Vows of religious men and women
_____ 3. Mother Seton
_____ 4. Charism
_____ 5. Saint Benedict
_____ 6. The Liturgy of the Hours
_____ 7. Franciscans and Jesuits

Column B

a. Special gift for ministry
b. The daily prayer of the Church
c. Author of the Rule of Life used by many religious communities
d. Poverty, chastity, and obedience
e. Founder of the Sisters of Charity who directed some of the first Catholic elementary schools
f. Missionary orders that brought the Gospel to the United States
g. Motto of Saint Benedict

SUNDAY MASS

At the end of Mass each Sunday, you are sent forth with the charge, "Go in peace to love and serve the Lord." In response to this blessing, you say, "Thanks be to God." This Sunday at Mass, think about what you are being sent from Mass to do. What will you do this week to love and serve the Lord?

CONTENT KEYS

1. Jesus' followers plant the seeds of faith.
2. The Holy Spirit enables you to serve others.
3. Christian service bears fruit.

> You have tasted that the Lord is good. Come to him, chosen and precious in the sight of God.
>
> 1 PETER 2:3–4

THE OFFERING

In a village near Jerusalem, there lived a couple named Benjamin and Hanna. Though they were poor, they always thanked God for what they had.

One Sabbath, after saying the blessing, Benjamin broke off a piece of bread Hanna had made. When he tasted it, he said, "Hanna, this is wonderful. You should make an extra loaf for the next Sabbath, as an offering to God."

"What an excellent idea," she said. And the next week, she happily prepared two extra loaves.

Before dawn, Benjamin carried the loaves to the synagogue. He opened the Ark, the container in which the Scriptures were kept, and placed the loaves inside, praying that God would accept their humble offering.

When the custodian came into the synagogue, he noticed the wonderful aroma of fresh bread. Though he was surprised to find two loaves in the Ark, he knew exactly what to do. He took the loaves to two families in the village who had no bread. "This is a gift from the Most High to your family," he said as he delivered each loaf.

This continued until one morning the rabbi of the synagogue came early to pray. He wondered why Benjamin was putting loaves in the Ark, but said nothing. When he saw the custodian taking the loaves out of the Ark, he asked, "How long has this been going on?"

"Perhaps six months," answered the custodian.

"This is not right," said the rabbi. "It is silly for Benjamin to think God takes his offering, and it is wrong for you to let Benjamin think so."

"Follow me," said the custodian.

When the rabbi saw how pleased the poor families were to receive the bread, he understood. God had accepted the offering of Benjamin and Hanna.

Based on a Jewish folktale

1. **What did God do with Benjamin's and Hanna's offering?**
2. **What sacrifice did Hanna and Benjamin make in preparing their offering?**

ALL FOR GOD

God does not have a mouth and God does not need food. But God's people are often hungry. As Jesus said in *Matthew 25:45,* "Whatever you do to the least person, you do to me."

God does not have hands and feet. God depended on someone else to take the bread to the people who needed it. People who provide food for God's people are heroes, whether they bake the bread or give it to someone else.

There are many ways to be a hero. On this page and the next are stories of people who provided for the needs of others. In what way is each of these people a hero?

THE RESCUE

Something was wrong. Something was very wrong. The school bus was out of control, lurching across three lanes of traffic on the busy highway. The kids riding to school that morning screamed as they were thrown against the windows of the bus. Larry Champagne rushed up the aisle of the bus. The bus driver was slumped on the floor. Larry grabbed the wheel and hit the brakes of the bus just before it slammed into the guardrail once again. The bus stopped. A few of the nineteen students on the bus had minor injuries, but all were safe. The bus driver, who had suffered a major stroke, survived, too.

"I didn't do anything special," eleven-year-old Larry told the reporters who interviewed him on the St. Louis evening news. In fact, Larry was surprised that everyone was making such a fuss over him.

What Makes Larry a Hero?

A Change of Heart

Mrs. King, my next door neighbor, had a cute little dog named Prince. Every afternoon, Allison, Mrs. King's niece, took Prince for a walk. I called to Allison once, and she said "Hi" politely, but she kept on walking.

A few days later, Allison stopped at our sidewalk. I could hear Prince yipping at her heels, ready to go. "My aunt told me that you like Prince," Allison called. "Would you like to go for a walk with us?"

"Sure," I said, "Great! Just let me tell Gramps. I'll be right there."

When I got back from walking Prince, Gramps was waiting for me. He was real excited that I had made a new friend. But when I told him she went to Saint Matthew's School, I could tell he was upset. Gramps was Catholic, but he has never forgiven God for my being born blind. He had not been back to church in twelve years.

But Allison was so friendly that Gramps soon started going on the walks with us. I could tell he was glad she was my friend. She had a way of making you see the hopeful side of things.

Last Sunday, Mom and I decided to join Allison's family at Saint Matthew's for Mass. When we told Gramps what we were doing, he asked if he could join us. What do you think about that?

PLANTING SEEDS

Your friendliness, kindness, and helpfulness are Good News for other people. You may be the person who shows God's love to someone. You may be the only Gospel somebody reads. What are some ways that you can plant seeds of faith in other people's lives?

What Makes Allison a Hero?

BLOOM WHERE YOU'RE PLANTED

Thea Bowman grew up in Mississippi. Thea developed a strong faith from her family and from the Franciscan sisters who taught her.

When Thea Bowman became an adult, she joined the Franciscan Sisters of Perpetual Adoration. Sister Thea was to become a book in which others could read the Gospel in big, bright letters.

Toward the end of her life, bone cancer made Sister Thea too weak to stand. Even though she was forced to sit in a wheelchair, Sister Thea never stopped proclaiming God's love. She sang powerful Gospel songs. She preached. She was a living witness that faith can overcome prejudice and even death. Her eyes were bright and her voice strong as she shared her message with many audiences.

Sister Thea asked the bishops of the United States to reach out to African-American people, Catholics and non-Catholics, in love and justice.

"Today," she said, "we're called to walk together in a new way toward the land of promise. If we walk and talk and work and play together in Jesus' name, we'll be who we say we are, truly Catholic."

Throughout her life, Sister Thea planted little seeds of peace and justice. These seeds are still growing, reaching and teaching people like you.

Sister Thea Bowman knew the joy of living the Gospel, serving, and loving. In the end, she said, "What matters is how I love, how I laugh, how I listen, and how I communicate the Good News."

A GREAT HARVEST

In the Gospel of Mark, Jesus tells a parable about the way the Holy Spirit works in the lives of Christians.

This is how it is with the kingdom of God; it is as if a man were to scatter seed on the land and would sleep and rise night and day and the seed would sprout and grow, he knows not how. Of its own accord the land yields fruit, first the blade, then the ear, then the full grain in the ear. And when the grain is ripe, he wields the sickle at once, for the harvest has come.

MARK 4:26–29

Even when it seems difficult to follow Jesus—when someone you love is blind to the truth, when you're not sure what to say or do, when you face prejudice or serious illness—there's Good News.

The seed of the kingdom of God has been planted in you. It grows and bears rich fruit, even when you don't know how or why. If you make room for the Holy Spirit, if you keep growing in your faith, the green sprout of hope will break through even the hardest soil.

- The seed of the kingdom grows in people who profess the Creed. It grows when you study the Bible, when you pray, when you care about others.
- The seed of the kingdom is watered in Baptism and strengthened in Confirmation. It is nourished in the Eucharist. Reconciliation and Anointing help the seedling grow straight and tall and healthy.
- The seed of the kingdom bears fruit wherever God's People serve: in Marriage and Holy Orders, in religious life, in lay ministry. The fruit of the seed is holiness, justice, peace, and unending love.

WHAT'S IN IT FOR ME?

When you're trying a new food or trying a new sport, you don't really know what you're getting into. You don't know if you'll like it. You don't know what commitment you will have to make. You don't know whether you will be able to do what is required of you.

Following Jesus by acting with Christian love and service is also an unknown. You don't know what will be required of you or if you will like it. You just have to jump into the unknown and find out for yourself. But you will never have to wonder if your efforts will be in vain. Jesus promised that God will see what you do and will be proud of your efforts.

GOD'S GUARANTEE

Jesus offered all of his followers a promise that they would celebrate with God in this world and in the next. These are some of his promises.

- You will rejoice in your good works, like a farmer who has a good crop.
- Your efforts will produce results—even though you may not always see them right away.
- You will grow in faith, hope, and love.
- You will receive the peace of Christ, a peace that the things of this world cannot give.
- You will be happy in times of difficulty.
- You will have the gift of eternal life.

1. **What fruits of God's kingdom do you see in Sister Thea's life?**
2. **What things make it hard for you to follow Jesus?**
3. **What are some of the rewards of following Jesus?**
4. **Where do you see the seed of the kingdom growing in your home, school, parish, or community?**

A farmer plants the seed and trusts that God will provide rain and sun. You have to trust God, too. Some seeds—like the fire poppy and the bristlecone pine—must be seared by a forest fire before they can begin to grow. Whether good things or bad things are happening to you, God is there for you. Think of one thing in your life right now that is hard for you or that you are worried about. Ask Jesus to help you grow through this problem and bring good out of your efforts.

WITH YOUR FAMILY

Share your promise to grow in faith with your family. Ask family members to help you keep your promise during the summer by reading the Bible, praying, and sharing the Eucharist together.

MY PROMISE

Jesus made a promise to you. Are you ready to promise to follow Jesus in return? Write your own promise describing how you will continue to follow Jesus as you grow in faith. Be specific.

THANK GOD

GROUP 1: I will bless the Lord at all times, God's praise shall be ever in my mouth. Let my soul glory in the Lord, the lowly will hear me and be glad.

GROUP 2: Glorify the Lord with me, let us together praise God's name. Look to God that you may be radiant with joy, and your faces may not blush with shame.

GROUP 1: When you are in trouble and call out, the Lord hears, and from all your distress you will be saved. The angel of the Lord will camp around you and deliver you.

GROUP 2: Taste and see how good the Lord is, happy are you when you run to the Lord. The great grow poor and hungry; but those who seek the Lord want for no good thing.

Based on PSALM 34

CATHOLICS BELIEVE

1. The seed of God's kingdom is planted in the followers of Jesus.
2. The work of Christian service bears fruit in the kingdom.

KNOW

Choose **T** if the statement is true. Choose **F** is the statement is false.

T F   1. Acts of Christian service can be small, like seeds.

T F   2. You can always see the good that will come from your actions.

T F   3. The Holy Spirit helps the kingdom of God grow.

T F   4. You will never face any obstacles in your life.

T F   5. You can continue to grow in faith, hope, and love.

T F   6. Jesus compared the kingdom of God to a seed that grows and bears fruit.

T F   7. The fruit of Christian service is holiness, justice, peace, and love.

SUNDAY MASS

With your class, share a special offering with your parish family. You could make a banner, collect money and food for the parish food pantry, or clean up an area of the parish grounds. Show the parish that you are ready to follow Jesus.

The Game of Sacramental Life

Play this game with three of your classmates or take it home and play it with friends and family members.

MATERIALS

- Vocation cards. Make three slips of paper that say "marriage," one that says "priesthood," and one that says "religious life."
- Markers for each player
- One die

DIRECTIONS FOR PLAYING GAME

- Throw the die. The player who rolls the largest number starts. Turns move clockwise. Each player rolls once each turn.
- Follow any special instructions on the space you land on. If it says "Go back to Reconciliation," go back to the last Reconciliation square you passed.
- Stop at each "STOP" sign to celebrate a sacrament.
- When you get to the Marriage/Holy Orders/Religious Life square, accept the vocation card chosen for you by the person on your right.
- Play until everyone goes to heaven.

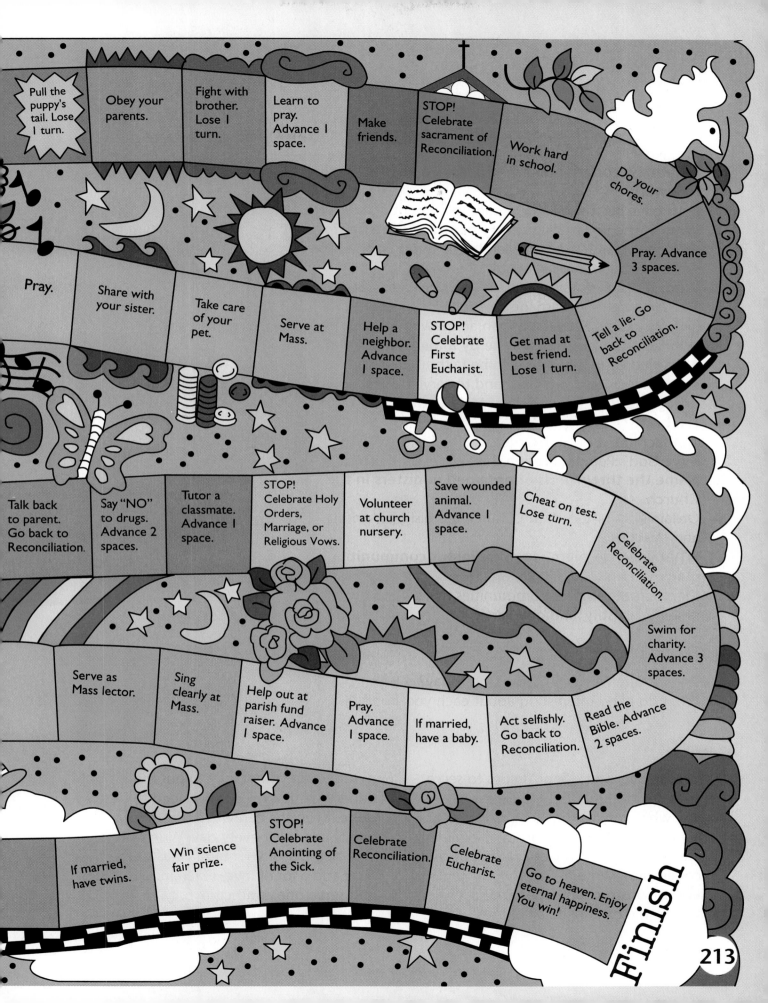

Pull the puppy's tail. Lose 1 turn.

Obey your parents.

Fight with brother. Lose 1 turn.

Learn to pray. Advance 1 space.

Make friends.

STOP! Celebrate sacrament of Reconciliation.

Work hard in school.

Do your chores.

Pray. Advance 3 spaces.

Pray.

Share with your sister.

Take care of your pet.

Serve at Mass.

Help a neighbor. Advance 1 space.

STOP! Celebrate First Eucharist.

Get mad at best friend. Lose 1 turn.

Tell a lie. Go back to Reconciliation.

Talk back to parent. Go back to Reconciliation.

Say "NO" to drugs. Advance 2 spaces.

Tutor a classmate. Advance 1 space.

STOP! Celebrate Holy Orders, Marriage, or Religious Vows.

Volunteer at church nursery.

Save wounded animal. Advance 1 space.

Cheat on test. Lose turn.

Celebrate Reconciliation.

Swim for charity. Advance 3 spaces.

Serve as Mass lector.

Sing clearly at Mass.

Help out at parish fund raiser. Advance 1 space.

Pray. Advance 1 space.

If married, have a baby.

Act selfishly. Go back to Reconciliation.

Read the Bible. Advance 2 spaces.

If married, have twins.

Win science fair prize.

STOP! Celebrate Anointing of the Sick.

Celebrate Reconciliation.

Celebrate Eucharist.

Go to heaven. Enjoy eternal happiness. You win!

Finish

213

LEARNING

1. **What new commandment did Jesus give his followers?**
Jesus gave his friends a new commandment of love.

2. **What is the vocation of every baptized Christian?**
All followers of Jesus are called to the ministry of service through the sacrament of Baptism.

3. **What does the sacrament of Marriage celebrate?**
The sacrament of Marriage celebrates a covenant of love that exists between a man and a woman.

4. **What are the promises made by a married couple?**
A married couple promises to be faithful, to accept children lovingly from God, and to serve others.

5. **What does the sacrament of Holy Orders celebrate?**
The sacrament of Holy Orders celebrates the call to serve God's People through the ordained ministry.

6. **Name the three kinds of ordained ministers in the Church.**
Ordained ministers of the Church are bishops, priests, and deacons.

7. **What vows do members of religious communities make?**
Members of religious communities make vows of poverty, chastity, and obedience.

PRAYING

Group 1: Take as your model the sound teaching you have heard, in faith and love in Christ Jesus.

All: We will!

Group 2: Treasure the rich gift of faith with the help of the Holy Spirit who dwells in you.

All: We will!

Group 3: You are charged solemnly in the presence of God and in Christ Jesus: Proclaim the Word, whether it is convenient or inconvenient.

All: We will!

Group 4: Perform the work of one who brings the Good News of the kingdom: Fulfill your ministry!

All: We will!

Based on 2 TIMOTHY 1:13–14, 4:1–5

ASKING

1. What is one way I can serve God today?
2. What do I find interesting about each vocation?

LIVING

Many of your best opportunities to serve others are at home. But you may not know what you can do to help. Here's a solution, and a way for your whole family to serve one another. Get a large can (like a coffee can). Write "I Can Help!" on a piece of construction paper and glue the paper to the can. Invite all of the members of your family to put in slips of paper describing jobs that need to be done. Keep the can where the whole family can see it every day. When you or any member of your family has a little time and a lot of love, reach in, pick a slip, and serve one another joyfully.

I Am a Catholic

CONTENTS

MEET SAINT TERESA

Greetings! My name is Teresa. I lived in the sixteenth century in the beautiful walled town of Avila, Spain. When I was a girl, I loved to read the lives of the saints. My brother Rodrigo and I ran away from home once. Our plan was to go to a faraway land to die for the faith. I have to tell you that it was not love of God that was guiding us. We just figured that dying for the faith was the quickest way to enjoy the wonderful things awaiting us in heaven. We didn't die though—our uncle Francisco found us and took us home.

When I was a teenager, I was very proud of my good looks. I spent a lot of time fixing my hair. I wore the latest styles, and I had a favorite perfume. I always had lots of fun laughing and joking with my friends. One day, I saw a statue of the suffering Jesus. I wanted to turn away, but I couldn't. I just cried. Then I prayed. I told Jesus how much I loved him. That simple, prayerful moment was a turning point in my life.

When I was twenty years old, I left home again—this time to become a Carmelite nun. I got very sick in the convent. I prayed to Saint Joseph for help, and I got better. Saint Joseph became my special friend after that, and I turned to him whenever I needed help. He never let me down!

FIXING THE OLD

When I was forty-eight years old, I found my mission in life. I saw that the sisters of my convent had lost the spirit of our order. I wanted to renew that spirit with more quiet prayer, fasting, and penance. Some of my sisters agreed with me. We fixed up a small house to live in. When we moved there, some of the other nuns were angry. They and the townspeople made fun of us. They thought I was a troublemaker. But I had more determination than most. Besides, I knew in my heart that this was what Jesus wanted us to do.

When my sisters and I were working on renewing the Carmelite order, we did many penances. Instead of fashionable dresses, we wore rough brown robes. We went barefoot, even in winter. We ate no meat. We fasted, except on feast days. Actually, sometimes we didn't have much food because we were so poor. We slept on straw mats, and we worked hard. But we were happier than ever because our way of life brought us closer to Jesus.

Some people were very suspicious of me and my sisters. Once, when I was traveling to start a new convent, my host prepared a roast partridge for my dinner. It seems that someone wanted to catch me breaking one of my own rules. I certainly did not want to hurt my host's feelings, so I said, "There is a time for partridge and a time for penance."

SHARING GOD'S JOY

I was a very busy woman, no doubt about it. But I managed to write eleven books, some poems, and thousands of letters. You see, when I finally learned to trust Jesus in all things, I was so filled with joy that I wanted to share that joy with others. I wrote the story of my life so that others would know what God had done for me. In my books on prayer, I tried to help others know Jesus the way I did.

Usually I would write late at night. It was my only free time. I sat at a small oak table, an oil lamp burning. Sometimes my quill pen just seemed to race across the paper. The words in my heart wanted to come out faster than I could write.

A church official once criticized me. He said that I taught theology as if I were a Doctor of the Church. Well, in 1970, Pope Paul VI declared me a Doctor of the Church. I had a good laugh over that one!

CELEBRATE

ADVENT

The word advent means "coming." Advent is the four weeks before Christmas. In the Sunday Gospels during Advent, John the Baptist calls on people to prepare the way of the Lord. At this time of year, people all around the world are preparing for Christmas.

Decorations and Christmas trees are displayed everywhere. Christmas carols are played on the radio, and special programs are shown on television. People send cards to tell their families and friends that they care about them. Everyone is eager to celebrate Jesus' birth.

Advent Masses tell people to prepare *in their hearts* for the coming of Jesus. These passages from Scripture are read during Advent:

- Isaiah 2:1–5 and 35:1–6
- Matthew 3:1–2, 11:2–11, and 24:37–44
- Luke 1:39–45 and 3:10–18
- Romans 15:4–9

Look up the passages for yourself and learn the meaning of the season.

CHRISTMAS

Giving gifts for Christmas is a way to show that Christ has come into the world. Gift-giving is a worldwide custom.

- In Germany, Christ-bundles containing fruit, candy, toys, clothing, paper, pencils, and books are often given for Christmas.

The year is filled with times to have feasts and times to do penance. On feast days, my sisters and I sang and danced. I hope you know how important it is to celebrate together.

218

- In England, presents are exchanged on Boxing Day, the first weekday after Christmas. This custom started long ago when the parish priests used all the money collected in the alms boxes to buy gifts and food for the poor.
- In Holland, children save coins all year in clay pigs, which can be opened only at Christmas.
- In Spain, in South America, and in parts of Canada, children believe that on Christmas Eve, the Christ Child comes with angels to put up the Christmas trees and to bring presents.
- In the United States, children look forward to a visit from Santa Claus, another name for Saint Nicholas.

LAS POSADAS

Catholics in Spanish speaking countries celebrate the Christmas season with the *Las Posadas*. The word *Las Posadas* is Spanish for "the inns." The custom is based on the Bible story of Mary and Joseph's search for shelter in Bethlehem.

For nine nights, families gather outside the church. From there, they march with lighted candles throughout the neighborhood, singing hymns and reciting prayers. Two children, carrying statues of Mary and Joseph, lead the procession. Each night the families go to different houses.

At the front door of each home, the fathers sing a song of Saint Joseph, asking for shelter for his pregnant wife and himself. At several houses, the procession is turned away. When the procession arrives at the final home, they are welcomed in. The statues of Mary and Joseph are set to

rest on a table or small altar. On Christmas Eve, the nativity scene is completed by placing an infant Jesus in a manger.

Following the Christmas Mass, the community joins together for a fiesta with special foods and games. The custom in Mexican and Central American communities is to celebrate with piñatas filled with candy.

219

CELEBRATE

LENT

Take up your cross and follow me.
MARK 8:34

Christians fast and do penance during Lent, giving up rich food and special treats. On the days before Ash Wednesday, people have great feasts. They eat all of the foods that they do not eat during Lent—meat, butter, eggs, fat, and sweets. That is why the day before Ash Wednesday is called Fat Tuesday, or (in French) Mardi Gras.

The forty days of Lent remind Christians of Jesus' forty days alone in the desert. There he prepared himself to do his public work. The days also remind Christians of the forty years the Israelites spent wandering in the desert before they reached the land God had promised them.

Catholics do not eat meat on Ash Wednesday and on Fridays during Lent. Many people choose to give up certain pleasures during Lent, such as soft drinks or candy, and give the money they save to help the poor. Lent is a season for prayer and for being kind and generous to others.

EASTER

Easter is the most joyful time of the Church year. The joy comes from a belief in the new life Jesus gives to all. The word *Easter* comes from the old German name *Oestra*. Oestra was the goddess of dawn and of the spring. The word was used by Christians to mean a time of new birth in Christ. Easter has many symbols.

• **The Butterfly:** The caterpillar wraps itself in a cocoon and seems to die. Then, after a while, the cocoon breaks open and a butterfly is born.

- **The Egg:** The egg will soon hatch, and a new chick will hop out. The egg is a sign of Jesus breaking from the tomb to a new life.
- **The Peacock:** Every year, peacocks lose their tall feathers, but they always grow back more beautiful than before. This regrowth is a symbol of the hope Christians have in new life.
- **The Crocus:** The crocus is a spring flower. It blooms in spring while there is still snow on the ground. It is a sign of the triumph of new life over the death of winter.

PENTECOST

After Jesus' death, his followers were frightened. They weren't sure what to do. One day, Peter, James, John, Thomas and the other close friends of Jesus were sitting around and talking. They were sad because Jesus had left them for good. But they were also excited, because they remembered Jesus' promise to send them a Helper. Suddenly, the disciples knew that the Helper, the Advocate, had come. No one knocked at the door. They did not see anyone, but they knew that the Holy Spirit was present. This happened fifty days after Easter, and we call this day Pentecost.

CELEBRATE

SPECIAL TIMES

The sacraments are signs and celebrations of God's love and saving power, or grace. Through the sacraments, you help build up God's kingdom on earth and strengthen the unity of God's People.

1. **Baptism** You are freed from sin, you're given the new life of grace, and you become a member of the Church.
2. **Confirmation** The gift of the Holy Spirit strengthens the baptized person to live as Jesus did.
3. **Eucharist** Jesus is truly with you in the consecrated bread and wine.
4. **Reconciliation** Through a priest, God forgives sins.
5. **Anointing of the Sick** A priest anoints a person who is sick and offers God's healing and forgiveness.
6. **Marriage** A man and a woman promise to live forever as husband and wife.
7. **Holy Orders** The Church ordains deacons, priests, and bishops to teach, to lead, to celebrate, and to care for God's Family.

THE MASS

The Mass is the center of Catholic life and worship. Every Mass follows a set pattern, or order. It is not hard to learn that order. The following outline will help you learn and remember the flow and pattern of the Mass.

1. **Gathering for Mass**
   a. The people gather in the name of Jesus. The priest enters with the ministers. Usually the people sing during the entrance procession.
   b. The priest greets the people.
   c. All ask for forgiveness and mercy and sometimes sing a song of praise.
   d. The priest says a gathering prayer.

2. **Liturgy of the Word**
   a. Someone reads from the Hebrew Scripture.
   b. Everyone responds with verses from a psalm.
   c. Someone reads from the Christian Scriptures.
   d. The people sing or say "Alleluia!"
   e. The priest or the deacon reads from the Gospel.
   f. The priest or the deacon gives a homily—
      a message about God's Word in everyday life.
   g. On Sundays, all join in reciting the Nicene Creed.
   h. All pray for the needs of God's People and share a greeting of peace.

3. **Liturgy of the Eucharist**
   a. People carry gifts of bread and wine to the altar.
   b. During the Eucharistic Prayer, the bread and wine become the Body and Blood of Jesus.
   c. At the end of the Eucharistic Prayer, all say "Amen!"
   d. All may raise or join their hands and join in the Lord's Prayer.
   e. If they have not done so earlier, the people share a sign of peace.
   f. The people receive the Body and Blood of Jesus in Holy Communion.

4. **Dismissal**
   a. The priest reads a closing prayer.
   b. The priest blesses the people and sends them out to love and serve the Lord.

PRAY

PEOPLE OF PRAYER

Prayer is the door to the good things God has waiting for you. There are many different ways that you can pray.

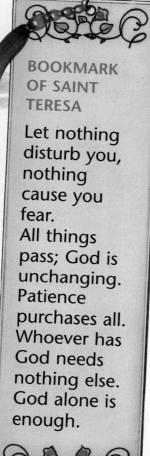

BOOKMARK OF SAINT TERESA

Let nothing disturb you, nothing cause you fear. All things pass; God is unchanging. Patience purchases all. Whoever has God needs nothing else. God alone is enough.

Prayer is friendly and frequent conversation with God. If you have not begun to pray regularly, for heaven's sake, don't miss out on such a great blessing!

PRAY BY YOURSELF

You can talk to God anytime and anywhere. You can pray aloud or quietly. Talk to God just the way you would talk to your parents or to a friend. Keep these ideas in mind.

Take time to talk to God.
Thank God for the gifts you have received.
Ask God for any help you need.
Tell God what you think and how you feel.
Be open to hear what God has to say.

PRAY WITH OTHERS

Christians often join together to pray. Sometimes that prayer is as simple as a mealtime blessing. It can be as full and rich as the celebration of the Mass. When you pray with others, keep these ideas in mind.

Join in. Don't sit silently.
Listen to others when they witness to God's love or read from the Scriptures.
Keep your heart in what you are doing.
Don't let you mind wander away.
Try to mean the words you pray.

PERSONAL PRAYER

You already know how to pray. Almost every time you open your mouth you use one of the ways people talk to God!

1. Greeting: "Hi, there!" "How are you doing?" "Good morning." Greeting other people is so common that it is considered very rude to walk up to somebody and start talking without a greeting. When you begin prayer, you greet God.

2. Praising: "Nice jeans!" "You have a great voice." "I love the poem you wrote." Nothing brings a smile to someone's face faster than a few words of praise. Praising God is a very natural thing to do.

3. Telling Stories: "Have you heard what happened to Janet?" "Did you hear about a big snowstorm?" "Let me tell you about the new video game." Everybody loves a story. You can tell God stories about what is happening to you.

4. Remembering: "Remember when Grandma gave Bobby those bunny pajamas?" "I'll never forget my tenth birthday party!" "Remember the time you were sick and Uncle Joe came to read to you?" When you pray, you can remember the wonderful things God has done for you.

5. Giving Thanks: "Thanks for the help on my science project." "Thanks for letting me come along with you." "I really appreciate the chance to take my test over." Gratitude is the fuel that drives relationships. Saying thank you to God is an easy way to pray.

6. Apologizing: "Mom, I'm sorry I'm late. You must have been worried." "I didn't mean to break the chain on your bike." "Forgive me for forgetting the money I owe you." Being sorry is an important part of human relationships. It is important to ask God for forgiveness, too.

7. Asking: "Can you help me wash dishes?" "I need help with the groceries!" "Would someone please let the dog in?" You are used to being asked to lend people a hand. You can ask God to lend you a hand anytime you want.

CATHOLICS PRAY TO THE BLESSED TRINITY

SIGN OF THE CROSS

In the name of the Father,
and of the Son,
and of the Holy Spirit.
Amen.

GLORY TO THE FATHER

Glory be to the Father,
and to the Son,
and to the Holy Spirit;
As it was in the beginning,
is now and ever shall be,
world without end.
Amen.

CATHOLICS PRAY TO GOD THE FATHER

THE LORD'S PRAYER

Our Father, who are in heaven, holy is your name. Your kingdom come; your will be done on earth as it is in heaven. Give us this day our daily bread, and forgive us our trespasses as we forgive those who trespass against us. And lead us not into temptation, but deliver us from evil. Amen.

CATHOLICS PRAY FOR FORGIVENESS

ACT OF CONTRITION

My God, I am sorry for my sins with all my heart.
In choosing to do wrong and failing to do good, I
have sinned against you whom I should love above
all things.
I firmly intend, with your help, to do penance, to
sin no more, and to avoid whatever leads me to sin.
Jesus Christ suffered and died for us. In his name,
dear God, forgive me.
Amen.

CATHOLICS PRAY FOR VIRTUE

ACT OF FAITH

O my God, I believe that you are one God in three Divine Persons: Father, Son, and Holy Spirit. I believe that your Divine Son became man and died for our sins, and that he will come again to judge the living and the dead. I believe these and all the truths that the Catholic Church teaches, because you have revealed them, who can neither deceive nor be deceived.
Amen.

ACT OF HOPE

O my God, relying on your almighty power and infinite mercy and promises, I hope to obtain pardon of my sins, the help of your grace, and life everlasting through the merits of Jesus Christ, my Lord and Redeemer.
Amen.

ACT OF LOVE

O my God, I love you above all things with my whole heart and soul, because you are all-good and worthy of all my love. I love my neighbor as myself for the love of you. I forgive all who have injured me and ask pardon of all whom I have injured.
Amen.

CATHOLICS HONOR MARY

HAIL MARY

Hail Mary, full of grace; the Lord is with you.
Blessed are you among women, and blessed
is the fruit of your womb, Jesus.
Holy Mary, Mother of God, pray for us sinners,
now and at the hour of our death.
Amen.

ROSARY TIMES

Here are the times in the lives of Jesus and Mary
that you can remember while saying the rosary.

Joyful Times
1. Mary learns she is to be God's Mother.
2. Mary visits her cousin Elizabeth.
3. Jesus is born in Bethlehem.
4. Mary and Joseph take Jesus to the Temple.
5. Mary and Joseph find the young Jesus in the Temple.

Sorrowful Times
1. Jesus prays in the Garden of Gethsemane.
2. Jesus is beaten.
3. Jesus is crowned with thorns.
4. Jesus carries his cross.
5. Jesus dies on the cross.

Glorious Times
1. Jesus is raised from the dead.
2. Jesus ascends into heaven.
3. The Holy Spirit comes to the Apostles.
4. Mary is taken to heaven.
5. Mary is called Queen of Heaven and Earth.

CATHOLICS PRAY ALWAYS

MORNING PRAYER

Almighty God, you have given us this day. Strengthen us with your power and keep us from falling into sin, so that whatever we say or think or do may be in your service and for the sake of your kingdom. Amen.

EVENING PRAYER

Lord, watch over us this night.
By Your strength, may we rise at daybreak to rejoice in the resurrection of Christ, your Son, who lives and reigns forever and ever. Amen.

BLESSING BEFORE MEALS

Bless us, O Lord, and these, your gifts, which we are about to receive from your bounty, through Christ our Lord. Amen.

GRACE AFTER MEALS

We give you thanks for these and all your gifts, almighty God. You live and rule forever. Amen.

FAMILY PRAYER

Heavenly Father, you have given us a beautiful example in the Holy Family of Jesus, Mary, and Joseph. Give us openness to your Spirit, so that we may follow through in the practice of family virtues.
Strengthen our bonds of love. Grant us the courage to reach out to others and to do your will. Amen.

Lots of saints were mothers and fathers, teachers and nurses, priests and sisters, monks and nuns, kings and queens. Saints are people just like you.

SAINTS AND STORIES

Did you know that a homeless beggar could become a saint? It's true. Saint Benedict Joseph Labre did. There are saints from just about every walk of life.

Saint Luke was a doctor.
Saint Clement was a baker.
Saint Isidore was a farmer.
Saint Catherine of Bologna was an artist
Saint Catherine of Genoa was a hospital administrator.
Saint Thomas More was a lawyer.
Saint Felicity was a slave.
Saint Ambrose was a governor.
Saint Ignatius was a soldier.
Saint Martin de Porres was a barber.
Saint Joseph was a carpenter.
Saints Tarcisius, Cecelia, Maria Goretti, Aloysius, and Stanislaus Kostka were teenagers.

THE DANCING SUN

Portugal, like the rest of Europe, was torn apart by World War I. In the midst of that war, a miracle happened near the small town of Fatima.

Every day, Lucia dos Santos, who was eleven years old, and her cousins nine-year-old Francisco Marto and seven-year-old Jacinta Marto took their families' sheep out into the country to graze. On Sunday, May 13, 1917, the children were playing while the sheep grazed nearby. Suddenly, the children came face-to-face with a beautiful lady who seemed to be standing on top of a small evergreen tree. She was dressed all in white.

The lady told them she was from heaven and that she would come again. The lady appeared to the children on the thirteenth of each month for six months after that. Each time, she asked them to pray the rosary and to make sacrifices for peace. Each month, more and more people came to watch the children. Many did not believe that these poor children were seeing someone from heaven.

October 13, the day of the last visit, was chilly and rainy. But more than seventy thousand people were waiting with the children. That day, the lady told the children that she was Mary, the Mother of God. After Mary was gone, the sun danced in the sky and then spun like a top shooting off lights of rainbow colors. People in nearby towns witnessed the miracle of the dancing sun.

SAINT LAWRENCE

Lawrence was a young deacon in the early days of the Church. He lived in Rome. At that time, Christians were being persecuted for their faith. When the pope, Sixtus II, was arrested, he told Lawrence to sell some Church property and to give the money to the poor. When the Roman emperor Valerian heard about this, he thought the Church must be very rich. So he ordered Lawrence to turn over to him the treasures of the Church. Lawrence asked for a little time to gather the treasure. Valerian gave him three days. After that time, Lawrence appeared at the emperor's palace. With Lawrence were poor people, the blind, the crippled, lepers, orphans, and widows. "These," Lawrence said to Valerian, "are the real treasures of the Church." On that very day, Valerian had Lawrence put to death. Lawrence died praising God and forgiving those who were putting him to death.

JESUS IS THE WAY

Did you ever have a real tough math problem to do or a new swimming stroke you wanted to learn? Maybe you tried very hard, but you just couldn't quite get it right. You needed a teacher, a coach, a parent, or a friend to show you how to do it. Jesus, said, "I am the way." Jesus can show you how to live. The closer you get to Jesus, the more on track you'll be. Learn what Jesus says to you.

1. Let your light shine before others, so that they may see your good deeds and glorify God.
2. Make peace with others before you bring your gift to the altar.
3. Love your enemies. If someone hurts you, don't strike back. Pray for those who hurt you.
4. If you forgive others their trespasses, your heavenly Father will forgive you.
5. Depend on God for everything you need.
6. Seek to know what God wants you to do.
7. Ask and it will be given to you; seek and you will find; knock and the door will be opened to you.
8. Treat everyone the way you would like to be treated.
9. Store up treasures in heaven, where no thieves can break in and steal them.
10. Take up your cross and follow me.
11. Peace be with you. My peace I give to you.
12. Love God with your whole heart, with your whole mind, with your whole soul, and with your whole strength.
13. Love others, as I have loved you.

LIVE BY THE BOOK

The Bible and the teachings of the Church will show you how to live. Reading the Bible and studying about your faith will help you know how to be a good follower of Jesus.

THE TEN COMMANDMENTS

Since the time of Moses, people have tried to live according to the Ten Commandments. Jesus himself was raised to observe the Ten Commandments. The commandments talk about actions—mostly about what you should not do.

1. I am the Lord, your God. You shall not have other gods besides me.
2. You shall not take the name of the Lord, your God, in vain.
3. Remember to keep holy the Sabbath day.
4. Honor your father and your mother.
5. You shall not kill.
6. You shall not commit adultery.
7. You shall not steal.
8. You shall not bear false witness against your neighbor.
9. You shall not covet your neighbor's wife.
10. You shall not covet anything that belongs to your neighbor.

THE BEATITUDES

Jesus knew that what a person feels and thinks is also important. He taught his followers that attitudes count just as much as actions. This teaching of Jesus is called the Beatitudes. The attitudes you learn from Jesus and from the Church will guide you to genuine and never-ending happiness.

- Blessed are the poor in spirit, for theirs is the kingdom of heaven.
- Blessed are they who mourn; God will comfort them.
- Blessed are the meek, for they will inherit the land.
- Blessed are they who hunger and thirst for righteousness, for they will be satisfied.
- Blessed are the merciful, for they will be shown mercy.
- Blessed are the clean of heart, for they will see God.
- Blessed are the peacemakers, for they will be called children of God.
- Blessed are they who are persecuted for the sake of righteousness, for theirs is the kingdom of God.

EXAMINE YOUR CONSCIENCE

At night, before you go to bed, take a few minutes to think about how well you have followed Jesus. Ask yourself these questions.

❶ In My Heart

- Do I love God?
- Do I love my family and friends?
- Do I love God's gift of life?
- Did I pray today?
- Did I wish only good for others?
- Did I forgive others?
- Did I respect myself?
- Did I respect others?
- Did I show respect for the property of others?
- Were my thoughts pure?
- Was I jealous or envious?

❷ In My Words

- If I hurt someone, did I say "I'm sorry?"
- Did I tell the truth?
- Did I spread gossip?
- Did I use hurtful or indecent language?
- Did I tease or say mean things?
- Did I say God's name with respect?
- Did I thank God for all good things I have?
- Did I make peace?

❸ In My Actions

- Did I fight or hurt others?
- Did I help others?
- Did I obey my parents and teachers?
- Did I cheat?
- Did I take anything that is not mine?
- Did I share?
- Was I kind to others?

BELIEVE

WHAT CATHOLICS BELIEVE

It is important to have the right language to talk about your faith. When you use the right words, you can share your faith with others. This list of statements will give you answers to some questions you may have. You may not understand everything the statements mean right now. But as you grow older, you can seek and learn more and more about your Catholic beliefs.

I loved learning about God and about the teachings of the Church. Try to learn as much as you can, too. It will bring you real happiness every day of your life.

1. The seven sacraments are words and actions instituted by Jesus to share his life with the members of his Church, so that all can grow in holiness.

2. Baptism, Confirmation, and Eucharist are the sacraments by which new members are initiated into the Catholic Church.

3. Reconciliation and Anointing of the Sick offer the healing power of Christ to the believing community.

4. The Trinity is three Persons in one God: God the Father, God the Son, and God the Holy Spirit.

5. Jesus Christ is God made flesh. In Jesus, God became human—a Divine Person with a human nature. This is called the Incarnation.

6. Jesus saved all from evil, sin, and death.

7. The Church is the People of God.

8. The habit of personal prayer is important for those who follow Jesus.

9. Those who follow Jesus are responsible for their actions, and they always try to choose what is right.

10. Every human being is created in the image of God. Human life is sacred and must be protected from conception until death.

11. All Christians are called to use their gifts and talents in the service of God. Some Christians receive a special call from God to serve the Church as priests or religious.

12. All will be judged at the end of life. They will be rewarded or punished depending on their love and faithfulness. The reward is called heaven. The punishment is called hell.

CHURCH RULES

1. Take part in the Eucharist every Sunday and holy day. Don't do unnecessary work on Sunday.

2. Receive the sacraments frequently.

3. Study the Good News of Jesus Christ.

4. Follow the marriage laws of the Church.

5. Support the People of God.

6. Do penance at certain times.

7. Support the missionary efforts of the Church.

HOLY DAYS

Feast of Mary, Mother of God—January 1
Ascension of Jesus—forty days after Easter
Assumption of Mary—August 15
Feast of All Saints—November 1
Immaculate Conception—December 8
Christmas Day—December 25

THE GIFTS OF THE HOLY SPIRIT

Wisdom	Understanding
Right judgment	Knowledge
Courage	Reverence
Wonder and awe	

CORPORAL WORKS OF MERCY

Feed the hungry.
Give drink to the thirsty.
Give clothes to those who have none.
Shelter the homeless.
Visit the sick.
Visit the imprisoned.
Bury the dead.

SPIRITUAL WORKS OF MERCY

Help the sinner.
Teach the ignorant.
Counsel the doubtful.
Comfort the sorrowful.
Bear wrongs patiently.
Forgive injuries.
Pray for the living and the dead.

THE APOSTLES' CREED

I believe in God, the Father almighty, creator of heaven and earth.

I believe in Jesus Christ, his only Son, our Lord. He was conceived by the power of the Holy Spirit and born of the Virgin Mary. He suffered under Pontius Pilate, was crucified, died, and was buried. He descended to the dead. On the third day he rose again. He ascended into heaven, and is seated at the right hand of the Father. He will come again to judge the living and the dead.

I believe in the Holy Spirit, the holy catholic Church, the communion of saints, the forgiveness of sins, the resurrection of the body, and the life everlasting.
Amen.

NICENE CREED

We believe in one God, the Father, the Almighty, maker of heaven and earth, of all that is seen and unseen.

We believe in one Lord, Jesus Christ, the only Son of God, eternally begotten of the Father. God from God, Light from Light, true God from true God, begotten, not made, one in Being with the Father.

For us and for our salvation he came down from heaven: by the power of the Holy Spirit he was born of the Virgin Mary, and became man.

For our sake he was crucified under Pontius Pilate; he suffered, died, and was buried. On the third day he rose again in fulfillment of the Scriptures; he ascended into heaven and is seated at the right hand of the Father. He will come again to judge the living and the dead, and his kingdom will have no end.

We believe in the Holy Spirit, the Lord, the giver of life, who proceeds from the Father and the Son. With the Father and the Son he is worshiped and glorified. He has spoken through the Prophets.

We believe in one, holy, catholic, and apostolic Church. We acknowledge one baptism for the forgiveness of sins. We look for the resurrection of the dead, and the life of the world to come.
Amen.

BELIEVE

THINGS TO REMEMBER

1. What is the Blessed Trinity?
The Blessed Trinity expresses the mystery of three Persons in one God: Father, Son and Holy Spirit.

2. Why is God called the Creator?
God is called the Creator because God made the world and breathed life into every human being. God continues to care for all creation.

3. What are the Nicene and Apostle's Creeds?
The Apostles' Creed and the Nicene Creed are statements of Catholic belief.

4. Who is Jesus?
Jesus is true God and true man. He is the only Son of God and the savior of the world.

5. What is the Paschal Mystery?
Jesus' death, resurrection, and promised return is the Paschal Mystery.

6. What happened on Pentecost?
On Pentecost, the Holy Spirit came to the Church as a gift from God. The Holy Spirit is the Church's Helper and Advocate.

7. What are the four marks of the Church?
The Church's four marks are one, holy, catholic, and apostolic.

8. What are sacraments?
Sacraments are signs and celebrations of God's power and love. Catholics share in God's life through the grace of the sacraments.

9. What are the sacraments of initiation?
The sacraments of initiation are Baptism, Confirmation, and Eucharist. Through these sacraments, a person belongs to Christ and to the Church.

10. What are the sacraments of healing?
Reconciliation and Anointing of the Sick are the sacraments of healing. They both offer the peace and healing of God's forgiveness.

11. What is the Liturgy of the Word?
The Liturgy of the Word is the part of the Mass when the Word of God in Scripture is proclaimed.

12. What is the Liturgy of the Eucharist?
The Liturgy of the Eucharist is the part of the Mass when the sacrifice of Jesus is remembered and made present.

13. What do Catholics share in Holy Communion?
In Holy Communion, Catholics share Jesus, the Bread of Life, and his gift of peace.

14. What are all followers of Jesus called to do?
All followers of Jesus are called to the ministry of service through the sacrament of Baptism.

15. Where is the kingdom of God found?
The kingdom of God is found in the followers of Jesus.

GLOSSARY

Advocate A name for the Holy Spirit; Latin for "the One who speaks up for us, the One who takes our side."

Annunciation The feast that honors the angel's announcement to Mary, that she was to be the Mother of the Lord.

Anointing of the Sick The sacrament in which the Church cares for the sick and continues the healing work of Jesus Christ.

Apostle A close friend and follower of Jesus; one who is sent to do the work of the kingdom.

Apostles' Creed A profession of faith based on the teaching of the Apostles.

Baptism The sacrament of initiation that gives new life, washes away sin, and joins one to the Christian community.

Beatitudes Short sayings of Jesus about how to live in God's kingdom.

Belief Trust or confidence in a person or thing.

Believe Having a firm religious faith, willing acceptance of a teaching or statement of faith.

Bishop The leader or shepherd of a diocese; the highest level of Holy Orders.

Blessed Sacrament A name for Jesus present in the Eucharist.

Blessed Trinity A name for the one God who is Father, Son, and Holy Spirit.

Bread of Life A title Jesus uses in John's Gospel; the Eucharist.

Canonization The official process by which saints are honored.

Catechumenate A period of time spent in study and prayer in preparation for Baptism.

Catholic A word that means "universal, open to everyone."

Celibate Remaining unmarried in order to devote one's life to ministry.

Chastity The virtue of respecting God's gift of sexuality according to one's state in life.

Chrism Perfumed olive oil, blessed and used in the sacraments.

Christ A title for Jesus that means "the anointed or chosen one of God."

Church From the Greek word that means "belonging to God"; the Church is first of all the assembly, the Christian community, and only secondly the building in which they gather.

Commandment A rule or law meant to help people do God's will.

Commitment A solemn promise or intention to be faithful to a person, a work, or a belief. The followers of Jesus are committed to carrying out his mission.

Communion A word that means "union with"; a name for receiving Jesus Christ in the Eucharist.

Confession Telling one's sins to the priest in the sacrament of Reconciliation.

Confirmation The sacrament of initiation that seals and completes Baptism by strengthening you in the Holy Spirit.

Conscience The gift of God that helps you see the difference between right and wrong.

Consecrated Made holy, dedicated to God. Both persons and things may be consecrated.

Contrition Sorrow for sin combined with a sincere promise to do better.

Conversion The willingness to turn away from what is wrong and to turn toward what is good.

Council A formal gathering of bishops for the purpose of discussing and clarifying the teaching of the Church.

Covenant A sacred and loving promise of relationship.

Creation Everything made by God.

Creed A prayer or profession of faith made up of statements of belief; from the Latin, "I believe."

Deacon An ordained minister who helps the priest and the bishop serve the Christian community; the first level of Holy Orders.

Devotion Faithful love shown through prayers and actions.

Diocese A portion of the universal Church made up of a number of parishes in a certain area, led by a bishop.

Disciples Followers of Jesus; from the Greek word for "learners."

Easter Vigil The liturgical celebration, including the Service of Light, the Service of Readings, and the celebration of Baptism, that takes place on Holy Saturday evening.

Encyclical A letter written by the pope to the whole Church about matters of Catholic belief and behavior.

Eucharist The sacrament of Jesus' presence in Holy Communion; the Mass. The Eucharist is a sacrament of initiation. The word *eucharist* means "thanksgiving."

Evangelist Someone who brings Good News; the Gospel writers are called Evangelists.

Faith The gift of believing and trusting in God through the Church.

Fasting and penance Practices that train Christians to follow Jesus.

Father The name Jesus used for God, to show that God cares for all people like a loving parent.

Fidelity The solemn promise of lifelong faithfulness in Marriage.

Gifts of the Holy Spirit Qualities given to the Christian in Baptism and Confirmation.

Gospel The New Testament accounts of the life and teachings of Jesus. The word *gospel* means "Good News."

Grace A share in God's life and friendship.

Greeting of Peace The gesture of welcome and forgiveness you exchange before receiving Communion.

Heaven Being with God forever.

Hebrew Scriptures The Jewish sacred writings which contain the story of God's loving relationship with Israel. In Christian Bibles, the Hebrew Scriptures are contained in the Old Testament.

Holiness Being like Jesus. All people are called to be holy.

Holy Orders The sacrament that celebrates the call to serve God's People through the ordained ministry of deacon, priest, or bishop.

Holy Spirit The Gift of the Father and the Son, who is present in the Church.

Homily A brief talk or sermon that helps to break open and explain the Word of God.

Incarnation The belief that Jesus, the Son of God, became human and was born of Mary.

Initiation The process of joining or belonging to a group or community. Baptism, Confirmation, and Eucharist are sacraments of initiation into the Christian community. Adults are welcomed into the Church through the Rite of Christian Initiation of Adults.

Inspired Filled with the Holy Spirit.

Judgment When Jesus comes again to bring the kingdom of God. This is called the Last Judgment. At the time of death, each person also faces a personal judgment; for the Christian, judgment is a source of hope, not fear.

Justice The virtue of treating all people, especially those most in need, with fairness, respect, and mercy.

Kingdom of God A name for God's power and love working in our lives. Jesus came to proclaim the kingdom of God, and to invite all people to follow him into the everlasting kingdom.

Laity All baptized persons who have not received the sacrament of Holy Orders.

Law of Love Jesus' new commandment: "Love one another as I love you" *(John 15:12)*.

Lectionary The book that contains the Scripture readings used in the Liturgy of the Word.

Lector A person who performs the liturgical ministry of proclaiming the Scriptures in the Liturgy of the Word.

Light of the World A title Jesus uses for himself. Jesus told his followers that they were to be the light of the world.

Liturgical Year The cycle of seasons and feasts celebrated by the Church.

Liturgy The Church's public worship, including the Mass and the sacraments; from the Greek for "work of the people."

Liturgy of the Eucharist The part of the Mass when you give thanks and take part in Jesus' death and resurrection, and share his body in Communion.

Liturgy of the Hours The daily prayer of the Church, composed of psalms, prayers, and readings from Scripture; also called the Divine Office.

Liturgy of the Word The part of the Mass in which the Scriptures are read and explained.

Lord's Supper A name the early Christians used for the celebration of the Eucharist.

Manna The Hebrew word for the miraculous "bread from heaven" with which God fed the Israelites in the desert *(Exodus 16:4–35)*.

Marks of the Church Signs of the presence of the Holy Spirit; the Church is one, holy, catholic, and apostolic.

Marriage The sacrament that celebrates the covenant between a man and woman to be faithful; to have children, if possible; and to serve others.

Martyr A person who dies for his or her faith; from the Greek word for "witness."

Meditation Quiet mental prayer.

Messiah The Hebrew word for God's anointed or chosen One; the Savior promised by God. Jesus is the Messiah.

Ministry Loving service to others. In Baptism, every Christian is called to the ministry of service.

Miracle A supernatural sign of God's power and love. Jesus performed miracles to show God's goodness.

Mission The work each person is sent to do.

Missionary Someone sent to carry the Good news of Jesus to the world.

New Testament The part of the Christian Bible that contains the Gospels, the Acts of the Apostles, the Letters, and Revelation.

New covenant God's relationship with the followers of Jesus; the promise to open the kingdom of God to all people.

Nicene Creed The profession of faith said at Sunday Mass.

Old Testament The part of the Christian Bible that contains the Hebrew Scriptures and other sacred writings from before the time of Jesus.

Ordained A word that means "appointed," or "set in order."

Parable A special kind of teaching story, often with a surprise ending, used by Jesus to tell about God's kingdom.

Parish A local community of Catholics who gather to celebrate the Mass and the sacraments, to share the faith, and to serve the needs of the community.

Paschal mystery The death and resurrection of Jesus, the mystery of our faith.

Passion The arrest, trial, suffering, and death of Jesus, commemorated during Holy Week.

Passover The Jewish Feast of the Unleavened Bread that commemorates the Israelites' passage from slavery to freedom.

Pastor From the Latin word for "shepherd," the leader of a parish. Bishops are sometimes called pastors of their dioceses.

Penance A way to make up for sin and to practice making better choices, given by the priest in Reconciliation.

Penitential Rite The part of the Mass when we ask forgiveness for our sins from God and the community.

Pentecost The feast that commemorates the sending of the Holy Spirit; celebrated 50 days after Easter.

Pilgrim A person who travels for religious reasons. Such a journey is called a pilgrimage.

Pope The bishop of Rome and successor of Saint Peter; the head of the church on earth. The word *pope* comes from the Latin word for "father."

Prayer Communication with God. Prayer can be spoken, sung, or silent. It can be formal or spontaneous. The four purposes of prayer are adoration, thanksgiving, petition, and contrition.

Priest An ordained minister who has received the second grade of Holy Orders. The priest serves the community by sharing the Word and celebrating the sacraments.

Procession A kind of formal parade that is part of worship.

Prophet A person who calls others to follow God's Word and to be fair and just.

Psalm A sacred song used in worship. The Book of Psalms in the Bible is a collection of 150 of these songs.

Reconciliation The sacrament that celebrates God's forgiveness and reunites you with God and with the Church.

Redeemer A title for Jesus.

Religious communities Groups of men and women who make solemn promises to follow a life of prayer and service.

Repent To turn away from one's old life of sin and turn toward new life in Jesus.

Rite The formal words and gestures used in liturgical celebrations. The word *rite* also describes the many different traditions, rules, and ways of celebrating that are part of the Church. Most United States Catholics belong to the Roman, or Latin, Rite.

Sacramentals Objects that help you remember God's presence. Holy water, blessed ashes, palms, and candles are all sacramentals.

Sacraments Signs and celebrations of God's power and love. Through the sacraments, you receive grace—a share in God's life and friendship.

Sacrifice Something precious offered to God out of love and worship.

Saint A title meaning "one who is holy." All Christians are called to be saints.

Salvation God's great act of love and mercy, sending Jesus to save the world from sin and death.

Sanctifier A title for the Holy Spirit that means "One who makes holy."

Satan The biblical name for the devil.

Sexuality The quality of having been created male or female; the gift of God through which parents pass on life to their children.

Sin The condition of being separated from God and the community; the deliberate choice to do what is wrong.

Son of God The title given to Jesus to show that he is both God and man.

Son of Man A biblical title for the Messiah, used by Jesus to describe himself.

Soul God's gift of everlasting life, or spirit.

Spiritual Having to do with the spirit, or soul.

Stewardship Showing care for one another and for all creation.

Synagogue A Jewish house of worship and religious study.

Synod A gathering of bishops. At some synods, bishops representing all the countries of the world meet in Rome to advise the pope on important Church matters. Other synods are local or national.

Temple The central place of worship for the Jews, located in Jerusalem.

Ten Commandment The laws given by God to Moses on Mount Sinai as part of the covenant with Israel.

Tradition From the Latin word for "handing on"; the collected teachings of the Church.

Unleavened bread Bread made without yeast or leaven, used by the Jews for Passover and by Christians for the Eucharist.

Viaticum Holy Communion received at the time of death; from the Latin words for "food for the journey."

Virtue A practice that leads to goodness or holiness.

Vocation A call from God to serve others in God's name. Marriage, committed single life, priesthood, and religious life are all vocations.

Vows Sacred promises.

Witness To express one's beliefs in words and action.

Word of God The belief that God speaks to the Church in the Bible. Jesus is also called the Word of God.

Works of Mercy Practices that help bring about God's kingdom by serving others.

Worship Praise and honor given to God alone.

INDEX